YOUR DREAMS & WHAT THEY MEAN

A fascinating insight into the mysterious world of dreams showing how we can learn to understand and utilize their power in our daily lives.

By the same author
THE DREAMER'S WORKBOOK
FORTUNE-TELLING BY PLAYING CARDS

YOUR DREAMS
& WHAT THEY MEAN

How to Understand the Secret Language of Sleep

by

NERYS DEE

GUILD PUBLISHING LONDON

This edition published 1988 by
Guild Publishing
by arrangement with
Thorsons Publishers Limited

CN 9058

Printed in Great Britain by
Biddles Limited, Guildford, Surrey

To Bill
who made my dream come true

CONTENTS

INTRODUCTION

Dreams are as much a part of our lives as everything else we experience but unfortunately their importance and the role they play has been sadly neglected. Not only can they help us to understand ourselves, other people and those difficult situations in which we so often find ourselves, they show us glimpses of the future, solve our problems and help us heal ourselves, too. At the very least they are excellent topics of conversation, for whose interest is not roused when someone says, 'I had a very funny dream last night'?

We all dream, even those who insist that they never do. The difference between the dreamer and the supposed non-dreamer is that one remembers his dreams whereas the other does not. Since we sleep on average for one third of each day it means that by the time we are seventy-five years old we have slept for twenty-five of these years and for at least ten of them we have been dreaming. This is a lot of dreaming, but we still do not really know what a dream is nor, for that matter, what sleep is.

Dictionaries describe dreams as 'visions in the night' and leave it at that but this is only a vague description of what goes on, not what they *are*. Generally, we think of dreams as visual experiences but what of non-visual dreams? We have five senses and sight is only one of these. Added to this we have what is often called a sixth sense and this includes intuitiveness and psychic awareness. To the ancients dreams were messages from the gods and even from God

Himself but today they are regarded as emotional expressions from our innermost selves. Since dreams reflect life in all its many aspects from the mundane to the mysterious, both the beliefs of the ancients and those of modern psychiatrists are correct in their own way and from their different standpoints, for dreams are all things to all men.

As a dream analyst it is the dream I analyse, not the dreamer. To me dreams are highly personal messages from ourselves to ourselves so obviously the best person to interpret and understand them is the dreamer who created them. This, however, does not mean that someone else cannot discover the messages hidden in another's dream because they can. What they cannot do is to apply that message with its personal associations to the dreamer's own situation or circumstances. Only the dreamer can do this. As an example, the dream message that warns the dreamer of a person who owns, say, a blue car and has a tall tree in their garden means absolutely nothing to the interpreter but to the dreamer, who alone recognizes this person, it means everything. When interpreting dreams for others it is, therefore, very important not to impose our own association of ideas, collected through our own experiences in life, onto their dream messages.

The interpretation of dreams is only one aspect of the whole concept of dreaming. Dreams are potential sources of great wisdom and guidance and there is much we can do to delve into this enormous reservoir and so receive answers to problems, to order as it were. This is exactly what the ancients did five thousand years ago when they practised the art of dream incubation, so why not now? The incubation of dreams is simply a request made to ourselves, to God or to those universal forces once known as gods and goddesses. C. G. Jung called them archetypes. After all, we are transported nightly with the help of Hypnos, Morpheus and Hermes to the Land of Dreams. Dream incubation encompasses life in every respect so by having the right dream at the right time it can help with practical, down-to-earth problems just as easily as it can bring flashes of enlightenment and inspiration from heavenly heights.

Practice makes perfect so the more dreams we have the easier it becomes to understand them. With the help of a dictionary the meanings of signs and symbols can be discovered but no dictionary can do more than this. It cannot, for example, tell us whether a dream is literal, symbolic or a mixture of both and this is what we need to know first of all. Once an interest in dreams has been kindled, however, the rest is easy and even if that interest is only fleeting, like some of our dreams, the important thing is that we carry on dreaming and at least recognize and respect our dreams for what they are.

1

DREAMS THROUGH THE AGES

Dreams have intrigued mankind since the dawn of time and there have always been those around to interpret them. The Egyptians had Joseph, the Greeks had Plato and every Roman legion had its soothsayer to make sense of those nocturnal visions that crept uninvited into the minds of slumbering men. As well as dream interpreters they also had in those days special oracles and shrines where individuals could go to consult priests who dreamed for them or they could incubate or encourage their own dreams in order to receive that divine guidance.

One of the oldest recorded dreams is to be found in Mesopotamian literature and this prophesied a gloomy impending disaster. The hero who dreamed this described a huge tidal wave engulfing and swamping much of the face of the earth; in detail very similar to the biblical account of the Flood. The oldest dream book in the world, however, is thought to be a collection of Assyrian, Babylonian and Egyptian dream-lore collectively called *Artimedorous's Oneiro-Critica*. This was the only work of any consequence on dreams right up until the nineteenth century, by which time it had been translated from Greek into English and reprinted over thirty times. There is also an old Hittite prayer from long ago requesting the help of the powers that be in the following words: 'Either let me see it in a dream or let it be discovered by divination or let a divinely-inspired priestess or priest find out by incubation of a dream whatever it is I demand of them.'

Hebrew, Celtic, Greek, Arabic, Indian, Chinese, Japanese, French and Russian cultures all possess ancient records showing the important part dreams played not only in the lives of individuals but in shaping the heritage and destiny of these people as a whole. Religions, philosophies, the classics, history, politics, science and the arts all owe far more to the subtle power of dreams than is generally realized, and from a purely personal standpoint, what are our hopes, relationships and loves all about if not based on the magic of dreams?

Looking back over the centuries at certain dreams experienced by mankind, it is clear to see the effect these have had on history and on our way of life. Every type of dream possible has been experienced by the famous and the infamous and whether inventive or creative, warning or prophetic, many have been woven into the colourful histories of every nation on earth. Some dreams have been quite literal and self-explicit, needing no interpretation. The impact from these often set in motion a train of events that is still having an effect today and furthermore looks like continuing with this chain reaction for a long time to come.

Classical Dreams

To our ancestors dreams were regarded as messages from the gods and although these immortals no longer came down to earth men believed they still kept an eye on mortals in their struggle to understand what life was all about. The Assyrians, Babylonians and Sumerians had An-Za-Oar for their god of dreams who, they believed, held court in an underworld they called The Great Land. Here, he kept a legion of helpers whose job it was to pass on to sleeping man his divine instructions.

The Greeks had Zeus, father of the gods who, aided by Hypnos the god of sleep and his son, Morpheus, the god of dreams, sent warnings, inspirations and prophesies to humanity via Hermes, their winged messenger. Legends are rich in tales describing these visitations through the links which once existed between gods and man, a permanent reminder of which is found in our present day language of sleep and dreams bequeathed to us by these gods. When Hypnos tranquillizes us into sleep and we fall into the arms of Morpheus, who knows what revelations our dreams will bestow on us and to which far-off corner of the universe we will travel with wings on our heels, accompanied by our astral guide Hermes?

Perseus, we are told by Homer, had a dream showing him how to kill the dreaded gorgon with the snakey locks and upon whom to gaze meant instant death. It was Athene, the goddess of wisdom, who appeared to him in a dream and instructed him to polish his shield until it shone like a mirror. Once he had done this he was told to look only at the reflection of the monster, thus being able to kill it without even having to look at it directly.

When the plague afflicted the Greek army, through, we are told, Apollo's anger, an assembly was called to discover what should be done and in Homer's *Iliad* Achilles speaks thus: 'Come, let us enquire of some mantis or priest or interpreter of dreams, for dreams come from Zeus too, who may tell us why Phoebus Apollo is so wrath, if he has some complaint about prayer or hecatomb.'

Incubation of Dreams

Dreams and dream interpretations were forms of divination extensively used not only by the Greeks but long before them by ancient cultures all over the world. Like oracles generally, the purpose of these dreams was to determine the will of the gods and to receive their divine instructions. The seeking of dreams which would invoke the special powers of the gods is known as incubation and although ways of doing this varied in detail, in principle they were much the same throughout the Ancient World. Incubation is defined as sleeping in a sanctuary with the intention of receiving a dream-reply to a question asked of a god or goddess, having first performed the prescribed rituals. This was principally abstinence from sex, from eating meat and drinking alcohol and the giving of an offering to the Deity to be invoked.

Greek and Latin literature is full of examples, showing this form of communication with their gods. Many of the sacred Greek shrines were dream oracles so if a person had a problem, a visit to one of these was desirable. Delphi, the shrine of Apollo and the temple of Epidauros were two such famous places and it was to these that the sick went in hope that Asclepius, the god of healing, identified as Imhotep in Egypt, would come to them in their sleep. And when he did he usually brought the offer of practical advice in the form of herbal remedies and sometimes even dispensed instant cures. Priests and priestesses interpreted their dreams which contained the divine messages and these were revealed through a series of dreams, not usually just one. Votive inscriptions can be seen to this day testifying that many left the shrines completely cured.

Classical philosophers tried hard to explain the mysteries of sleep and dreams in terms of physical causes, as indeed the Common Sense theorists attempted earlier his century. Plato, for example, thought that the liver was the seat of dreams but in his famous work *Timaeus* he relents by saying that prophetic visions were received by the lower self, through the liver! Galen saw all dreams as health warnings, as did Cicero, but Aristotle believed them to be a mental effect from a physical cause. Democritus, on the other hand, considered them to be brought about by 'things floating in the atmosphere which attacked the spirit during sleep'. Pliny believed them to be entirely supernatural in origin but it was Hippocrates, the father of medicine, who probably came nearest to the truth when he said, 'Some dreams are divinely inspired but others are the direct result of the physical body.'

Although Greek philosophers of the day studied the cause of dreams, members of the public were more interested in their meanings for to them they were very important sources of information. Dream interpreters were therefore in great demand and consulted in much the same way as doctors are today. The difference was that these 'doctors' were expected to discover, from dreams, solutions to personal problems as well as remedies for the body.

The Gate of Dreams

Most dreams, however, were seen as either warnings or prophecies. A warning dream meant that trouble could be avoided if its message was acted upon, but nothing could be done about a situation if it was prophetic. To decide which of these a dream was, they used a method known as the Gates of Dreams. There were, apparently, two dream gates, one of ivory and one of horn. If a dream passed through the Ivory Gate it was a warning but if it passed through the Horn Gate it was prophetic. Dreams love puns, or at least our dreaming mind does, so it is not surprising that these symbolic gates were created from such a play on words. The Greek for ivory is 'elephas', also meaning to cheat and the Greek for horn is 'karanoo', also meaning to accomplish. Together, they represent that which can be averted and the inevitable!

Egyptian Dreams

Incubation of dreams was widely practised throughout Egypt from at least 4000 BC down to 2000 BC. According to a writer and explorer around AD 900 there was in existence then a village called Abusir on the fringe of the western desert to the south of Cairo and here could be seen the prison where Joseph had been kept at Pharaoh's order. It was a cavern-like place and within this was a seated statue of the Patriarch Joseph with an open book on his knees, covered with cabalistic signs. This 'prison', however, had originally formed part of the great complex known to the Greeks as the Asclepienion of Memphis, one of the greatest healing and oracular shrines of the Ancient World. The prison-cave itself was, in fact, the burial chamber of Imhotep himself.

The Butler and the Baker

Although the oracles themselves had long since been silent when Joseph was imprisoned here the gods of Egypt still remained and haunted the place. It was little wonder, therefore, that the butler and the baker, the two fellow prisoners and servants of Pharaoh, had their prophetic dreams which Joseph so accurately interpreted for them in this sacred place.

Egyptian kings as well as Pharaohs had great respect for their dreams and believed that they bestowed divine guidance and protection upon them and their royal line of successors. Between the paws of the Great Sphinx there is a slab of pink granite upon which is inscribed the dream of one man who later became king. Whilst sitting in the shade of the Sphinx this man fell asleep and Ra, the sun god, appeared to him saying that he would one day be ruler of Egypt. When he awoke he looked at the Sphinx and saw that it was partially covered with sand and was in need of repair so he vowed that if his dream came true he would make it his business to keep it for ever in perfect order. A few years later his dream did come true and he became Thothmes IV. Remembering his promise he restored the Sphinx to its former glory and from that day to this it has always been well maintained and kept free from the drifting sands of the Sahara.

Apart from this inscription there are hieroglyphs covering many steles and monuments in Egypt, especially around the Shrine of Asclepius-Imhotep still recording fragments of forgotten dreams. Some of these inscriptions reveal actual dream-meanings which have survived to this very day as traditional, timeless interpretation. One reads, 'A bed on fire means your partner is unfaithful to you.' Another says, 'To see a dead oxen or cow means you will triumph over adversity or your enemies.'

Biblical Dreams
One of the richest sources of dreams from the ancient world comes from the Bible. In the Old and New Testaments there are over twenty well-documented accounts of dreams each offering in different ways divine guidance in the form of warnings and prophecies. These messages were so powerful that in retrospect it can be seen how, by acting upon the advice given, the dreamers actually steered the destiny of nations, and so, in many instances, altered the course of history.

Old Testament Dreams
Although modern-day evangelists cry out against divination, examples of this practice are nevertheless fully described in the Bible and it seems that the Israelites were well versed in these matters. There were, however, those who sought to prohibit all mention of oracles and this in the course of time became the dominant view of the final editors of the Old Testament. Divination associated with the prophets, earlier termed 'priestly oracular messages' became 'dreams inspired by God and His angels'.

When considering the Old Testament evidence concerning visual divination described as visions and dreams, we find that the

Hebrew word for 'vision' and for 'dream' is the same as 'to see'. Since visions and dreams in the Old Testament foresaw the future, they were, by definition, oracular, but biblical prophets, seers and dream interpreters were not classified as fortune or misfortune tellers; but what is there in a name? Not all dreams, however, were thought to come from Yahweh and as the passage in Jeremiah 13:25 shows, it was the distinction of a prophet to cry, 'I have had a dream, I have had a dream.' The inducing of dreams, known as incubation, was similar to that of the rest of the ancient world as is seen in 1 Kings 3. Here, Solomon follows the well-recognized custom when he sleeps and dreams in the hill shrine of Gideon. Another example is Samuel's night vision in 1 Samuel 3 where, it appears, it was a regular practice of his to sleep in the temple before the ark. And Jacob's dream at Bethel described in Genesis 28:10-22 gives detail of the ancient Canaanite sanctuary to which Jacob retreated in order to consult the oracle through sleep and dreams.

Dreams in the Bible fall into two distinct types: literal and symbolic. In one, God or His messenger speaks directly to the dreamer and gives him explicit instructions which need little or no interpretation. In the other, the messages are symbolic, appearing in the form of parables. These need considerable thought and interpretation before their meanings can be extracted. As biblical interpreters, it is Joseph and Daniel who emerge as the experts but all Hebrews were well versed in this art and had little trouble recognizing the messages contained in their dreams.

It is expressly stated in the Bible that God speaks to man in his dreams: 'For God speaketh once, yea twice, yet man perceiveth it not. In a dream, in a vision of the night when deep sleep falleth upon men slumbering upon their bed, then He openeth their ears and sealeth in their instructions.' (Job 33:14-16). The first dream in the Old Testament is an excellent example of this direct communication with its literal meaning abundantly clear! 'God came to Abimelech in a dream by night and said to him "Behold! thou art but a dead man for the woman thou hast taken is another man's wife."' (Genesis 20:3).

Jacob's famous dream involving the ladder which stretched down from heaven above to the earth below was both literal and symbolic, as the following extract shows: 'And he dreamed and behold a ladder set up on the earth and the top of it reached to heaven: and behold the angels of God were ascending and descending on it. And behold! The Lord stood above it and said "I am the Lord God of Abraham the father and the God of Isaac; the land whereon thou liest, to thee will I give, and to thy seed."' (Genesis 28:12). In a later dream just after departing from Labon, Jacob again receives God's instructions but this time via an angel. 'And the angel of God spoke unto me in a dream saying "Jacob", and I said, "Here I am". And he said, "Lift up thine eyes and see, all the rams which leap upon the cattle are ringstraked, speckled and grisled. Now arise and return unto thy land of thy kindred."' (Genesis 31:11-13). Acting as an intermediary, the angel's role in this dream is similar to that of Zeus's messengers, the underworld helpers of An-Za-Oar, the god of the Sumerians, Babylonians and the Assyrians and, in fact, bringers of dreams throughout the Ancient World.

Pharaoh's Dreams

The most colourful and memorable of all dreams in the Bible must surely be those of Pharaoh interpreted by Joseph, Jacob's favourite son. A prolific dreamer himself, Joseph was put into prison along with Pharaoh's butler and baker who during their internment had special dreams. Remembering that the prison holding these men was the famous burial tomb of Imhotep, situated amid one of the greatest oracular dreaming and healing shrines in Egypt known to the Greeks as the Asclepienion, it is not surprising they dreamed as they did.

And they dreamed a dream both of them, the butler and the baker of the king of Egypt, which were bound in prison. And Joseph saw them in the morning and they were sad and he asked, 'Whereof look ye so sad today?' And they told him, 'We dreamed a dream and there was no interpreter.' And Joseph said unto them, 'Do not interpretations belong to God? Tell me them, I pray you.' The butler told his dream to Joseph saying, 'In my dream, behold, a vine was before me, with three branches and it budded and blossom shot forth and the clusters brought forth ripe grapes. And Pharoah's cup was in my hand and I took the grapes and pressed them into his cup and gave it into

Pharaoh's hand.' 'The three branches', said Joseph to the butler, 'are three days; within three days Pharaoh will restore you to his service. And when he does, make mention of me, Joseph, and bring me out of this prison.' When the baker heard the interpretation was good, he too asked Joseph for the meaning of his dream, also featuring the number three. 'Behold,' he said, 'I had three white baskets on my head. In the uppermost one was baked bread and sweetmeats for Pharaoh and the birds did peck and eat this.' And Joseph answered: 'The three baskets are three days, yet within three days will Pharaoh hang thee on a tree and the birds shall eat thy flesh.' (Genesis 40:5-19). All this came to pass; the butler returned to Pharaoh's service, and the baker was hanged within three days. Joseph, however, remained in prison, forgotten. Two years went by, then Pharaoh had a dream that none of the wise men in Egypt could understand. Recalling his dream when in prison, the butler suddenly remembered the Hebrew Joseph and how he had correctly interpreted his and the baker's dreams. Joseph was sent for immediately. And Pharaoh said unto Joseph, 'Behold, I stood on the river bank and there came up out of the river seven fat kine; they fed in a meadow. And behold seven other kine followed them, poor and very ill-favoured and lean-fleshed, much as I had never seen in Egypt. And the ill-famed did eat up the fat kine.' Pharaoh awoke but later continued the dream which then showed seven full ears of corn and seven withered ears of corn and the seven withered ears of corn devoured the seven good ears. (Genesis 41:1-7).

The prophetic meaning Joseph attributed to this dream is well known – seven years of plenty followed by seven years of famine. What is not so readily realized is that the effects from this are still being felt to this day, showing it to be an excellent example of the subtle power certain dreams can have not only on the dreamer at the time but on others, generations later. Once having set in motion a sequence of events, as did Pharaoh's dream, a chain reaction started that will continue virtually forever.

The question is, what would have happened if Pharaoh had not had his dreams? The causal chain, however, did not start with his dreams but with the dreams of his butler and baker two years before. What, then, if they had not had theirs? To all intents and purposes, Joseph would not have interpreted them, so his reputation as a dream interpreter would not have reached Pharaoh's ears and he would therefore have languished in gaol; Egypt would not have stored up grain in readiness for the forthcoming seven-year famine; Joseph's eleven brothers and his father, Jacob later renamed Israel, would not have come down into Egypt to buy corn because it would not have been there. They would not, therefore, have been reunited with Joseph, their father's favourite son, whom they had abandoned in the desert some years previously, nor would they have settled in Egypt as they did. If the twelve brothers had not been reunited, there would not have been the Twelve Tribes of Israel and without the formation of this there would have been no exodus, no Promised Land, no line of David and no birth of Jesus as we know it. So, prophetic though Pharaoh's dream undoubtedly was in the short term, its shadow cast its long-term effect well into the future, far beyond those fourteen years covered by Joseph's prediction.

Moses and Solomon

Moses, we are told, was instructed by God to listen for His words in his dreams: 'Hear now my words. If there be a prophet among you, I the Lord will make myself known to him in a vision and will speak to him in a dream.' Centuries later Solomon also received a divine communication in a dream in which the Lord spoke to him: 'In Gideon the Lord appeared to Solomon in a dream by night and God said to him, "Ask what I shall give thee."' (1 Kings 3:5). In response to this, still within the dream, Solomon asks for help in discerning between good and evil. This pleases the Lord who, we read later, rewards Solomon with great riches.

Nebuchadnezzar and Daniel

Nebuchadnezzar, the King of Babylon, was another great biblical dreamer. His dreams troubled him greatly, added to which he tended to forget them on waking with a result that he was left with disturbing unconscious memories that he was unable to recall. Not surprisingly, requests for interpretations from his famous sorcerers and magicians failed, mainly because they were expected to produce the dreams themselves as well as their meanings. One dream in particular eluded the king as we read in Daniel 2:5. 'The king said to the Chaldeans, "This thing is gone from me. If ye will not make known to me the dream, with the interpretation thereof, ye shall be cut in pieces and your houses shall be made into dunghills."' The wise ones were quite unable to comply with this tough demand so the decree went out that they should all be put in prison and eventually slain.

Among these wise men was Daniel. Daniel, the Bible says, 'had understanding in all visions and dreams' and he soon convinced his guard of this fact. "I have found a man of the captives of Judah that will make known unto the king the interpretation of his dream,"' they said. Once in the presence of Nebuchadnezzar Daniel revealed that he had re-dreamed every detail of the king's dream: '"O King thy thoughts that came unto thee upon thy bed were these. Thou sawest a great image whose brightness was terrible. The image's head was made of fine gold, his breast and his arms of silver, his belly and his thighs of brass. His legs of iron, his feet part of iron and part of clay. A stone, cut without hands, smote the image upon his feet. Then was the iron, the clay, the brass, the silver and the gold broken to pieces and became as chaff on the summer threshing floor."' (Daniel 2:31-35). This, then, was the forgotten symbolic dream. The interpretation that followed revealed Nebuchadnezzar to be ruler of many kingdoms, himself represented by the golden head. Although kingdoms may come and kingdoms may go, Daniel assured him that his would go on for ever. The feet of clay, incidentally, now an inherited cliché in our everyday language, seem to have been nicely glossed over by Daniel, probably in order to please the tyrant king and save the lives of himself and his fellow prisoners.

New Testament Dreams

Dreams in the New Testament are fewer than in the Old but no less profound for all that. It was an angel who appeared in a dream to Joseph and gave him the following literal message: '"Joseph, thou son of David, fear not to take unto thee Mary thy wife for that which is conceived in her is of the Holy Ghost."' (Matt. 1:20). Later, the three wise men, after presenting their gifts of gold, frankincense and myrrh to the new-born child, received this dream warning: 'And being warned of God in a dream that they should not return to Herod they departed into their country another way.' (Matt. 2:12). Shortly after this Joseph received his second divine communication: 'And when they, the wise men, were departed, behold, the angel of the Lord appeareth to Joseph in a dream saying, "Arise and take the young child and his mother and flee into Egypt and stay thou there until I bring thee word: for Herod will seek the young child to destroy him."' (Matt. 2:13).

This Joseph did, remaining in Egypt until a messenger of the Lord visited him again: 'But when Herod was dead, behold, an angel of the Lord appeareth to Joseph in a dream and sayeth, "Arise and take the young child and his mother and go into the Land of Israel; for they are dead which sought the young child's life."' (Matt. 2:19-20). Here, then, is another example showing the long-term effect from a dream on the destiny of mankind. In the absence of this dream it is doubtful if the mother and child would have escaped the massacre of the innocents. How, one wonders, would history have shaped without the rise and subsequent influence of Christianity on world events?

Thirty years later Pilate's wife was to send the following message to her husband: 'When he, Pilate, sat down on the judgment seat his wife sent unto him saying, "Have thou nothing to do with that just man for I have suffered many things this day in a dream because of him."' (Matt. 27:19). This dream made no impact whatsoever on history for as literal as its message was, it was totally ignored. Who can say what would have happened if Pilate had exonerated Jesus, through this dream?

Early Christian Fathers

The early Christian fathers regarded dreams in much the same way as did the prophets of the Old Testament. Gregory of Nyssar in the fourth century AD accepted them as divine messages and even believed them to be mirrors of the soul which reflected the personality of the dreamer. In his work entitled *On Making Man* he wrote that from these visions it was possible to better understand and value one's true self. St Augustine used his dreams as channels of communication between himself, God and His angels, and he repeatedly requested them to maintain his 'chaste desires'.

Thomas Aquinas, a seer in the Old Testament sense, wrote extensively about the prophetic nature of dreams and suggested 'a single cause of both the dream and the event', a concept reminiscent of C. G. Jung's synchronicity.

Dreams in the Middle Ages

After the Tudor monarchs dreams were taboo, as far as the church was concerned. The fact that they had warned and inspired in the past, was conveniently forgotten by the officials of organized Christian religion and so dreams were classified along with all other esoteric arts as devil-inspired and devil's work. It is clear to see how this ignorant indoctrination made its mark on society generally, with the very word 'dream' being changed to mean not a vision in the night but a forlorn hope. People were soon saying, 'I would not dream of doing that', thus downgrading and reversing the whole concept and purpose of dreaming. By the nineteenth century, however, a glimmer of light appeared on the horizon and with the advent of Freud they slowly emerged as an acceptable and respectable experience again. This time, though, they took on a psychological image, not a religious or prophetic one. By doing this God and all other external sources of stimulation and inspiration responsible for dreaming insight and foresight were played down and overshadowed by Id, Ego and the Super-Ego, the new-found personal trinity. Today, as we near the end of the twentieth century those horizons have widened yet further so that now every conceivable aspect of dreams, from the deeply religious to the most mundane action-replay of a day's events are receiving serious and sincere consideration.

Dream Oracles in Japan

There are many accounts of dream oracles throughout medieval Japanese literature and from these we learn that there were places of incubation in both Shinto and Buddhist temples. One celebrated Shinto shrine at Usa in Kyushi was dedicated to the god Hachiman. Among the Buddhist temples three in particular were famous as dream oracles and dedicated to the Bodhisattva Kannon.

Whether the divinity to be invoked was Shinto or Buddhist the procedure for consulting the oracle was much the same. Having obeyed rules of abstinence in preparation, a journey was made to the holy site where an offering was made along with a vow that the proposed dreamer would stay there for a given time, in the belief of being granted an enlightening dream. Seven, twenty-one or one hundred days seem to have been the number of days necessary for this ritual, where each of these nights they spent sleeping in the principal hall as near as possible to the inner sanctum where the divinity dwelt. It was here that the long-hoped-for dream would come but often this did not happen until the very last night of the vigil.

Sickness was prominent among the troubles which impelled people to seek help from their dreams in this way and many of those who came in search of a cure found one. A fifteenth century collection öf stories known as Hasedra Reigenki describes the healing miracles achieved from dream communication with the gods. One of these tells of a man who, disfigured by leprosy, journeyed to Hasedra and after seven days and seven nights in seclusion dreamed that a boy appeared from the inner sanctum and said, 'Your sickness is very difficult to cure because it is due to karma from a past life. But Kannon has nevertheless commanded me to heal you.' The boy then licked the man all over and when he awoke in the morning he found himself clean and cured. Another man suffering from a terrible disease also made the pilgrimage to Hasedra and after one day and one night in the temple, dreamed that a boy appeared, again from the inner sanctum, and rubbed him all over with an ointment. Next morning his affliction had left him. In many of these stories the figure of a small boy appears from the holy of holies and performs apparently miraculous cures.

Problems other than health were solved by dream oracles, too. An inscription shows how a priest, unable to remember a very difficult passage by heart learned it in one night of dreaming. And a man, humiliated by his appearance, received confidence to face the world. Ladies reduced to states of despair and misery regularly sought this oracular help and all were transformed and sustained in thought on waking from nights of positive dreaming. There came pilgrims too, who simply wanted to know the future and here their dreams showed them visually what was to come.

their dreams showed them visually what was to come.

Before the coming of Buddhism, however, the Emperor was the principal dreamer and incubation of his dreams was part of his religious duties. His palace contained a special dream hall equipped with an incubating bed known as a Kamudoko. Once, when a terrible plague threatened his people the Emperor Sujin lay upon his Kamudoko in search of an answer which would help his people. This he received when his god Amonon Ushi appeared to him in his dream, telling him how to avert the calamity that was speedily sweeping the land. We are not informed exactly what the answer was, but it worked.

Tribal Dreams

North American Indians recognized the value of their dreams in helping them live peacefully together. The Huron and the Iroquios held regular dream festivals which lasted several days or even weeks, depending on the material collected. By pooling their dreams a distinct pattern emerged and this they used to help construct future tribal policy.

The Maoris in New Zealand and the Zulus in South Africa still pay particular attention to the pooling of dreams and their dream interpreters are appropriately called Head Men! Eskimos from the Hudson Bay and the Patani people as far away as Malaysia share the belief that during sleep the soul leaves the body and experiences in a special dream world. They also think it is very dangerous to wake anyone suddenly lest his spirit may not have time to return to his body and so it might be trapped for ever in limbo.

Collective and Communal Dreaming Today

Corsicans are very dream-conscious people and whole villages have a similar dream on the same night. It is as if there is a collective psyche that controls them telepathically during sleep and whatever or whoever this is, it has been going on for a long, long time and is still happening today.

The Temiar-Senois Tribe

The Temiar tribe, part of the Senois in Malaysia, are still

profoundly influenced both by the interpretation and the manipulation of dreams. According to their understanding, dreams are fragments of the personality consisting of psychic forces disguised as external, recognizable forms and although we see in this shades of C. G. Jung's personal and collective archetypes, these people knew all about this centuries ago. With this in mind their children are taught the importance of dreams from an early age and are encouraged to confront any bad spirits in their nightmares in order to master them before they grow up. As adults they pool their dream experiences which collectively reflect the future. The result of this is that they are able to foresee troubles and problems virtually before they arise. Crimes and violence are unheard of and as a society they are considered to be the most democratic and well-adjusted people on earth today.

These non-violent, self-reliant people were discovered by H. D. Noone in 1931 and since then they have intrigued western sociologists with their peaceful, balanced way of life. What so impressed Noone was the way they lived according to their own natural law. 'Where a man has given his labour he has a share of the harvest, though each man received not in proportion to his skill and labour, but according to his needs,' he said. Here seems to be the very essence of Karl Marx's dream where he suggested that 'each man should work to his full ability and take according to his needs'.

Unfortunately, humanity was not able to realize this dream of Marx's perfection but this is not surprising since humanity generally is not taught to dream as were the Temiar-Senois people. Communism worked for them and it is clear why!

Historical Dreams
Hitler
Not all dreams with long-lasting consequences are beneficial to human destiny, or so it would seem in the short-term view, as the following example shows. One bleak November night in 1917 the German and French forces were facing each other across the Somme locked in a deadly artillery bombardment. In one German bunker an exhausted corporal slept and had a dream, in the shape of a terrifying nightmare. In this, debris and molten earth

descended crushingly and suffocatingly upon him. Immediately, he awoke and dashed outside into the cold night air, thankful to discover it was only a bad dream. Seconds later, however, a French shell landed on the bunker he had just left and killed all the sleeping occupants. Realizing this dream had saved his life, the soldier thanked God, adding that he knew he had been rescued so that one day he could, in turn, save the Fatherland. The dreamer's name was Corporal Adolf Hitler. To contemplate the removal of Hitler from the scene in 1917 gives rise to nothing but pure speculation yet the temptation cannot be resisted to wonder what would have happened if he had not had that dream? Europe and the world would most definitely be a very different place today.

Alexander the Great

More than 2,300 years before Hitler had his infamous dream another ambitious world leader also had dreams and acted upon their messages. This was Alexander the Great. It is not surprising that when the city of Tyros was under siege, Alexander, educated by Aristotle, dreamed that a satyros – a nature spirit – danced on his shield. Aristander, his personal dream interpreter, translated this as a play on words so by dividing up and rearranging the letters in 'satyros' he revealed the encouraging message 'Tyros is thine'. This urged Alexander to renew his attack on the city with the result that it surrendered almost immediately.

Julius Caesar

Three hundred years later Julius Caesar, on whom it has been said Hitler modelled himself, was a great dreamer who, knowingly or unknowingly, acted out at least one of his dreams. Following a particularly vivid one in which he violated his own mother, he decided to take his army across the Rubicon, a small stream along the Cisalpine border. By doing this he found himself at war with the Senate for he had, in fact, invaded his own motherland. It is a pity, however, that he did not pay more attention to his wife's dream warning him of the danger he faced on the fateful Ides of March. Had he done so Calpurnia's dream would have remained a warning and not progressed into a prophecy that was fulfilled.

Joan of Arc

Many centuries later Joan of Arc was to dream that she was destined to save France. This, along with visionary day-dreams provided her with ingenious schemes which convinced the dauphin that she was quite capable of accomplishing this. In G. B. Shaw's play *St Joan* she is accused that her dream-voices come from her imagination. 'Of course,' she replied. 'That is how messages of God do come.'

Napoleon

Napoleon, another saviour of France, used his dreams to plan his military campaigns. On waking he would record his nightly impressions and then put them into practice, using toy soldiers in boxes of sand to work out each move and countermove.

Bismarck

When Napoleon died the future German statesman, Bismarck, was 6 years old. Noted for his extreme self-confidence, it was not known at the time that this was due to his dreams, mainly prophetic, experienced during his childhood and early military career. In a letter to Emperor William, Bismarck later wrote:

Your Majesty's communication encouraged me to relate a dream I had in the spring of 1863, during the worst of the days of struggle. I dreamed that I was riding on a narrow Alpine path, a precipice on my right and rocks on my left. The path grew narrower and narrower so that my horse refused to proceed and it was impossible to turn round or dismount. Then, with my whip in my hand I struck the smooth rock and called on God. The whip grew to an enormous length, the rocky wall dropped like a piece of stage scenery and opened out into a broad path with a view over the hills and forest like a landscape in Bohemia; there were Prussian troops with banners and even in my dream the thought came to me that I must report it to Your Majesty.

Encouraged by this reassuring message Bismarck stuck to his policies and succeeded in Prussia taking over the leadership of the German federation, so paving the way for Hitler's Fatherland.

It is clear to see how, to lesser and greater degrees, the dreams of military and political leaders have influenced and left their mark on thepages of history. How different it would be today if they had not acted upon messages and instructions given to them in their dreams!

Dreams and Literature

Before Freud described the dark battles going on in the minds of men and Jung unveiled the world of the collective unconscious filled with archetypes and symbols, poets and writers had long since discovered all this, and more. Their dreams had been mines of information on every subject under the sun, inspiring them to reflect on the profound psychological and paradoxical nature of man.

Expressing that confrontation of repressed savagery and open benevolence present within the authors and others, we find literary revelations that could easily have come straight from the confidential casebook of a present-day psychiatrist. The fears of hell and visions of horror were therefore recognized ages ago as aspects of one's darker unknown self and were never better summed up than by Plato in *The Republic* where he says, 'In all of us, even in good men, there is a lawless wild-beast nature which peers out in sleep.'

Neither Freud's generation, nor Freud himself, should have been surprised by his discoveries concerning man's true self if they had read earlier literature. The symbolic paradise dream, set in a personal garden of delight, was seen and written about in terms of compensation and wish-fulfilment, a long time before it received the analytical Freudian treatment. Tennyson's initial poems were filled with nocturnal landscapes inhabited by unapproachable maidens and nightingales, all seen and heard in a dream, and Keats with his dream gardens intruded regularly into 'some untrodden region of the mind'.

Shakespeare

Shakespeare must surely have been the greatest dreamer of all time. Throughout his work run themes and references to sleep and dreams conveying those states of reality and illusion between which we so often find ourselves trapped. In fact, Coleridge, in his lectures on Shakespeare, insisted that the only way to understand the Bard's message was to interpret his plays as one would a series of images and ideas created and embodied in a dream.

In *The Tempest* it is Caliban who dreams that, 'The Isle is full of noises and sounds and sweet airs that give delight and hurt not,' and he 'cries to dream again'. The character of the wise man Prospero suggests that life is but a dream: 'We are such stuff as dreams are made of and our life is rounded with a little sleep.' *The Tragedy of Macbeth* sees Lady Macbeth taking to sleep-walking, re-enacting her crimes and thus revealing that she possesses at least a grain of conscience. And she is reminded that, 'Sleep is the balm for hurt minds, nature's great second course.'

From *Hamlet*, the Prince of Denmark persuades us further with, 'To sleep, to sleep, perchance to dream – ay, there's the rub; for in that sleep of death what dream may come when we have shuffled off this mortal coil?' And in *A Midsummer Night's Dream* we find a world richly inhabited by timeless images representing real-life characters and shadowy figures and figments from another dimension. So it is with all Shakespeare's plays and really it is up to us to identify with one world or the other, the real or the symbolic, and usually it is the symbolic dream world that wins.

Bunyan and Coleridge

In a similar vein John Bunyan wrote *Pilgrim's Progress*. This is an allegory in the form of a dream and as such won him the title of the Immortal Dreamer. He was, however, less cordially known as the Mad Dreamer, too! Samuel Taylor Coleridge also experienced many creative dreams and the most fruitful of them was his famous *Kubla Khan*. In a lonely Somerset farmhouse Coleridge was suffering from a slight indisposition that caused him to sleep for several hours. During this time a series of images and sentences came to him and on waking he instantly began to write them all down, word for word. Unfortunately, he was interrupted by a man from Porlock who called on business, and as a result he lost several lines which he was never able to recall. In this we see the importance of recording a dream not only immediately on waking but without interruption, too.

Lewis Carroll

Charles Lutwidge Dodgson, better known as Lewis Carroll, was first and foremost a mathematician but in his famous story, *Alice in Wonderland*, he has Alice falling into her own dream world by entering a rabbit hole. Adventures and fears experienced throughout this story are hardly childish passing fancies nor are they really intended to amuse young minds, for this wonderland, full of outrageous characters, conundrums, surprises, threats and disappointments represents and relates to the mature, not the immature or infantile mind. Profound psychological and psychic observations disguised as reality and expeditions into other dimensions are all thrown into the melting pot of this fabulously symbolic dream, together creating an illusion ignorantly described by some uninitiated literary critics as 'nonsense verse'.

Robert Louis Stevenson

Robert Louis Stevenson seems to have been the best financially rewarded of all the dream essayists, novelists and poets. He, too, was fortunate in that he remembered most of his dreams and in his book *Across the Plains* he described how complete stories came to him during sleep. Each night he would pick up the fantasy-thread where he had left it the night before and carry on from there. This night-life, however, was so real that it troubled him greatly. The thought of leading a double life weighed heavily upon him, but this was to have far-reaching effects as he later wrote:

> I had long been trying to write a story on this subject, to find a body, a vehicle, for that strong sense of man's double being which must at times come upon and overwhelm the mind of every thinking creature. For two days I went about racking my brains for a plot and on the second night I dreamed a scene at the window, and the scene afterwards split in two, in which Hyde, pursued for some crime, took the powder and underwent the change in the presence of his pursuers.

This was the start of Dr Jekyll and Mr Hyde.

Walter de la Mare

Walter de la Mare, known as the visionary poet, wrote, among other things, an anthology of dreams. In this he begins by saying,

'A blatant beast is confined in the cellar of our unconscious and we must always be sure to possess the key that keeps it locked safely away.' This observation, taken from one of his dreams, is in contrast with the great innocence he described and saw in children. However, by recognizing this beast within he was at least in keeping with the thoughts of Plato and the beliefs of Freud.

Graham Greene
Graham Greene, winner of the 1981 Jerusalem prize for writing, is the latest in the long line of dream-inspired authors. He told an audience at the 1981 prize-giving that his books wrote themselves in the dead of the night. Apparently, he wakes up four or five times to record outlines of dreams that later form the basis of his novels. 'If I'm really working I re-read what I've written during the day before I go to bed and the problems are solved in my sleep.' He also went on to say that he kept a dream diary in which he recorded insights and story lines offered up by his unshackled mind!

Famous and Not So Famous Quotes on Dreams
Over the years the word 'dream' has changed to mean 'a hope' as well as a vision during sleep. In this context it often substitutes for the traditional meaning and gives depth and colour to otherwise unromantic statements. Not only have classical writers, poets and novelists reaped rewards by using dreaming in this way, so too have popular lyric writers. Recognizing the magic part dreams play in our love-lives they make full use of them in their songs, so here then, are just a few of the many quotes that have survived the centuries, some from as long ago as 1000 BC, and others as recent as today.

> The question was put to him, what is hope? And his answer was the dream of waking man.   Diogenes Laertius.

> While men are dreaming they do not perceive that it is a dream. Some will even have a dream within a dream. And so when the great awakening comes upon us, shall we know this life to be a great dream. Fools believe themselves to be awake now!   Chinese sage.

> Man is but the dream of a shadow.   Pythian Ode 8.

Once upon a time I, Chuang-tzu, dreamed I was a butterfly fluttering hither and thither, to all intent and purpose a butterfly. I was conscious only of following my fancies as a butterfly and was unaware of my individuality as a butterfly. Suddenly I was awakened and there I lay myself again. Now I do not know whether I was a man dreaming I was a butterfly or whether I am a butterfly now dreaming I am a man.

Swift as a shadow, short as any dream.   Shakespeare.

Napoleon, mighty somnambulist of a vanished dream. Victor Hugo.

The purification of politics is an iridescent dream. J. J. Ingalls.

But there is nothing half so sweet in life as love's young dream. Thomas Moore.

Forget that I remember and dream that I forget. Swinburne.

What I do and what I dream include thee, as the wine must taste of its own grape. Elizabeth Barrett Browning.

All that we see or seem is but a dream within a dream.   Edgar Allen Poe.

Don't ever try to go there, it's to dream of, not to find,
Lovely things like that are always mostly in the mind. Weaver.

A sight to dream of, not to tell. S. Taylor Coleridge.

A hope beyond the shadow of a dream.   John Keats.

Peace, Peace! He is not dead, he doth not sleep,
He hath awakened from the dream of life. Percy B. Shelley.

Many the long night I've dreamed of cheese, toasted mostly. R. L. Stevenson.

I slept and dreamed that life was beauty,
I woke and found that life was duty.
Was my dream, then, a shadowy lie?
Toil on sad heart, courageously,
And thou shalt find thy dream shall be,
A noonday light and truth to thee.   Ellen S. Hooper.

I dream of Jeannie with the light brown hair.   Song.

I'm dreaming of a white Christmas.   Song.

Dream lover put your arms round me.   Song.

Dreaming of you by the firelight glow.   Song.

Out of my dreams and into my arms.   Song.

I dream of you more than you dream I do.   Song.

What'y' wanna do, is make a dream come true.   Song.

Inventive Dreams
Elias Howe
Many inventors have to thank their dreams for their unique observations and discoveries, which later contributed to the development of our society and our way of life. In the nineteenth century a man called Elias Howe dreamed of natives throwing spears and each spear had an eye-shaped hole at its tip. On waking he immediately knew that he had solved the problem of where to put the hole in the needle in his latest invention. It was the sewing machine.

Fredrich August von Kekule
'Let us learn to dream, gentlemen,' was the opening remark and request Fredrich August von Kekule, Professor of Chemistry at Ghent, had to offer to a scientific convention in 1890. To explain this he related his own profitable experience from doing just that. Having struggled for some time without success to discover the molecular structure of trimethylbenzine, he went on to describe how the solution came to him in a dream:

I turned my chair to the fire and dozed. Again the atoms were gambolling before my eyes. This time the smaller groups kept modestly in the background. My mental eye, rendered more acute by repeated visions of this kind, could now distinguish larger structures, of manifold conformation; long rows, sometimes more closely fitted together; all twining and twisting in snakelike motion. But look! What was that? One of the snakes had siezed hold of its own tail and the form whirled mockingly before my eyes. As if in a flash of lightning, I awoke.

By the snake taking its tail into its own mouth, Professor Kekule was able to transform it into the closed chain or ring theory underlying the constitution of benzene, a discovery that later revolutionized organic chemistry.

James Watt

In a recurring dream James Watt found himself walking, time and time again, through a rain of heavy lead pellets. Eventually, this persistent scene crystallized into the message that if molten lead was dropped from a great height it would form into small spheres. He tested this out and found it did just that. He had discovered ballbearings and never had the dream again.

The French Professor

A similar experience although much less extensive in its later application was that of a French professor of biblical studies, who was having trouble in deciphering a particular Babylonian inscription. Despite consultations with authorities from all over the world the meaning still eluded him until one night the answer came to him in a dream. In this a Babylonian priest appeared to him and rearranged the order of the symbols. Instantly, it was transformed into a clear, coherent message.

Music

Many musicians have heard their compositions in their dreams and one of the most exciting examples of this concerns a sonata called The Devil's Trill. Giuseppe Tartini, the Italian composer, related to Lanlande, the astronomer, the origin of a sonata he had written when was twenty-one. This was recorded in Lanlande's account of his world travels and encounters. Apparently, Tartini dreamed he sold his soul to the devil and then he gave him his violin as well, to see if he could play it. This is what he told Lanlande:

> What was my astonishment when I heard him play with consummate skill a sonata of such exquisite beauty that it surpasses the most

audacious dreams of my imagination. I was delighted, transported, enchanted, I was breathless and I woke up. Seizing my violin I tried to reproduce the sound I had heard. But in vain. The piece I composed, *The Devil's Trill*, was the best I had written, but how remote it was from the one in my dream.

Dreams, Art and Surrealism

Biblical and historical dreams have provided artists with exciting subjects to paint since at least the eleventh century but it was not until the surrealist movement came along that dreams were psychologically captured in essence and in feeling. Surrealism, the name given to an artistic group in France in 1924, endeavoured to express dreams, the action of the unconscious mind, on to canvas. Although nightmares were no stranger to the imagination of the artist, Goya in particular excelling in this respect, none had tried to convey the atmosphere and symbolic message of the dream-experience until this time. 'Surrealism is based on a belief in the omnipotence of the dream,' said André Breton, often called the Pope of the Surrealist movement. Reaching its heyday in the 1930s the influence responsible for its emergence was clearly that of psychoanalysis. With Freud's emphasis on free association of ideas laced with sexual repression and Jung's symbolism, paintings appeared that shocked the world to its artistic roots. And even today there are those who, not caring to understand dreams, let alone art, dismiss this art as total rubbish.

Salvador Dali's paintings, with titles like 'The Persistence of Memory', 'The Birth of Liquid Desires', 'The Spectre of Sex Appeal' and 'The Great Masturbator', are clearly reflections of Freudian-type dreams. Melting telephones and furniture, watches, crutches, barren beaches, starved embryos and limp Oedipal figures eerily produce appropriate, dreamlike atmospheres of general dis-ease, un-ease and obsession. In contrast, Max Ernst, with his 'Robing of the Bride' and 'The Eye of Silver', fills his scenes with archetypal forests, blazing suns, bird-headed women, rocks towering to the sky, silent swamps and mysterious figures all very much in keeping with the traditional Jungian concept of dreams.

Other artists in this group went on to paint anxiety dreams, portraying strong feelings of fear and terror in one form or another. Hypnagogic dreams were a popular subject, too, showing images falling half-way between sleep and the waking state. Here to stay, surrealism certainly opened the door on our inner world and in so doing contributed in its own way towards a better understanding of art, ourselves and, of course, dreams too, for dreams are very much like paintings.

Dreamers, Visionaries and Geniuses

Leonardo da Vinci has been described as the greatest genius the world has ever known, and for good reason. He was a dreamer inspired to be a painter, a sculptor, an architect, a musical composer, a writer and an outstanding inventor. He designed an aeroplane and a submarine 500 years before they appeared in the twentieth century.

A genius is a visionary and a visionary is a dreamer. We are all dreamers and we may all be visionaries but we are not all geniuses. The difference between the da Vincis of this world and others is that they can pluck a thought or an idea that comes to them in the still of the night, in a dream and create from it reality. To them the true world is their inner world. Above all, they are good listeners, not only to other people but to that small, quiet voice within.

Dreams of the famous and infamous throughout the ages have without doubt helped to make history and shape our present way of life. In essence, however, their dreams are no different in any way from our dreams. We all have prophetic dreams, warning dreams and inspirational dreams just as they did, but if we do not accept them as sources of power and original thought, and acknowledge that we can obtain from them all information and solutions we can possibly need during our lifetime, they will be content to remain in the background like shy friends. Recognize them, however, and immediately they step forward and begin to put our house, the mansion of our soul, in order. But, like Professor Kekule said, we must first learn to dream.

2

DREAMS AND THE COMMON SENSE APPROACH

There have been many approach roads to dreams in the past and no doubt there will be many more in the future but one of the most recent to converge on them earlier this century was known as the Common Sense way. Ignoring the work of Freud and Jung this was based mainly on scientific evidence for the express purpose of proving once and for all that dreams were, in origin, nothing more than expressions from the physical body. The Common Sense theorists believed that indigestion, muscle fatigue, pain, fever and worry disturbed us during sleep and became manifest as dreams and nightmares.

Facts and Figures

Investigating dreams scientifically has been possible only since the invention of electrical monitoring devices over the past fifty years. This way is very different from the psychoanalytical approach which in itself includes psychological, philosophical, religious and mystical aspects. A practical investigation like this relies heavily on strictly controlled, repeatable experiments which will give the same results every time. Unfortunately, it was soon found that dreams do not conform and behave like conditioned performing animals for anyone, or for any thing, however sophisticated that thing might be. Statistics, therefore, varied from the start and although they demolished rather than established that which the

Common Sense theorists set out to prove, at least they added another dimension to dreams.

Brain Waves

At the beginning of this century physiologists discovered that nerves and muscles, including the heart muscle, gave off electrical impulses. And by the late 1920s they had found that the scalp also gave off similar wave motions. These, it was deduced, came from the brain and they called them Alpha and Beta waves. Since this time Delta, Theta, Mu, Gamma, Vertex, Spike and 'k' brain waves have been identified as well. To obtain tracings of these waves, electrodes are attached to places on the body and head where internal activity is best picked up; these are then intensified and transformed into wave motions which are penned onto graph paper or projected onto an oscilloscope. Depending on whether it is the heart or brain under investigation these tracings are known as electrocardiograms and electroencephalograms, in short ECGs and EEGs respectively. These, and other recordable physiological impulses and patterns are now collectively known as biofeedback data.

With the refinement of electronics came more and more detailed recordings of the brain's activity and by the 1950s two distinct sleep states, dreaming and non-dreaming, had been recognized. Since then there have been numerous contradictions of terms used to describe these two states as well as differences of opinions concerning results claimed by individuals. By the 1960s it was not, therefore, surprising to find that virtually every researcher used his own pet name for dreaming and non-dreaming sleep. These included 'deep and light', 'active and quiet', 'quiet and active', 'desynchronized and synchronized', 'high and low', and the most popular at the time, 'paradoxical and orthodox'.

NREM and REM Sleep States

Eventually it was noticed that rapid eye movements were associated with visual dreaming so at present non-dreaming and dreaming sleep are referred to as non-REM or NREM, and REM sleep states.

Early experiments carried out on sleeping volunteers in the

1960s used seven electrodes and much the same technique is still used today. Electrodes 1, 2 and 3 recorded cortical activity from the brain; 4 and 5 recorded eye movement; 6 recorded tone over the front of the neck and 7 recorded the heartbeat. The first surprise came when the subject closed his eyes. The cortical brain waves changed completely, as if in readiness for sleep. During sleep itself it was observed that the EEG could be divided into six distinct types which they labelled stages *A, B, C, D, E* and *F*.

Stage A tracing showed up much the same as when the subject was awake but had the eyes closed. *Stage B*, only minutes later, showed a distinct change from the first stage. The waves were slower and lower in voltage, and the subject's eyes drifted slowly. *Stage C*, about ten minutes later, showed that the slow waves were accompanied by 'sleep' spindles. There was virtually no eye movement so the subject was considered to be fully asleep. *Stage D* was similar to Stage C except that the waves were slower but higher in voltage. *Stage E* showed a higher voltage but still slow in motion. There was total cessation of eye movement. *Stage F*, however, brought a very different pattern indeed. The slow high voltage waves had gone and were replaced with fast low voltage waves; previously motionless eyes had become fully active and jerky; normal neck muscle tone was lost and the regular heartbeat recorded throughout stages A, B, C, D and E had now become irregular. It was, therefore, the characteristic 'rapid eye movement' in Stage F that eventually became known as the REM sleep state and stages A, B, C, D and E became Stages 1, 2, 3, 4 and 5, collectively known as the non-dreaming NREM sleep state.

During the night we progress through a series of sessions each lasting approximately 90 minutes. Throughout these the NREM and REM states alternate. We begin at stage 1 with NREM sleep and then move into further NREM stages 2, 3, 4 and 5. These are then followed by a phase of REM dreaming. It is this pattern that is repeated four, five, or even six times each night, depending on how much sleep we need. As we move towards morning, however, NREM sleep decreases and REM sleep increases. This accounts for the fact that we remember the dreams we have early in the morning best for it is just before we wake up that we have experienced our longest dreaming session.

This recurring 90-minute pattern may also account for the reason why insomniacs who wake in the middle of the night find it impossible to get to sleep again for at least an hour and a half. In other words, until they have missed out one complete 90-minute sleep session. The labelling of non-dreaming sleep, however, may not be quite as cut and dried as the terms suggest. The following dream laboratory observations show that during the NREM sleep state there is still plenty of brain activity going on so maybe it is a question of defining types of dreams more than types of sleep. Eighty per cent of volunteers wakened during REM sleep readily gave descriptions of visual scenes. Conversely, when they were wakened from NREM sleep only 7 per cent of them could describe a dream. But when the question was rephrased from 'Have you been dreaming?' to 'Were you thinking of anything?' 87 per cent in REM sleep recalled visual scenes and a surprising 74 per cent in NREM sleep recalled definite thinking activity, although not necessarily a visual dream.

Perhaps during NREM sleep we are sorting out our outer mundane problems, but in REM sleep we are dealing with inner symbolic matters. This was, in fact, confirmed to some degree back in the 1960s when the belief was that paradoxical sleep, now called REM sleep, produced the recall of more exciting, psychic adventures whilst orthodox sleep, now called NREM sleep, referred to everyday events.

Animals

Every proud owner of a cat or dog knows their pet experiences exciting dreams on the hearth rug. Scientific evidence, based not on domestic evidence but on rapid eye movement signals, has come to the same conclusion. These results, for what they are worth, state that fish never dream and birds spend only 0.5 per cent of their total sleep-time dreaming. This does not tally at all with the findings of non-scientific budgie owners. They say that Joey frequently talks in his sleep for 10 minutes or more and has to be stopped from carrying on. Apparently, what he says when asleep is clearer and more coherent than when he is awake. Maybe under laboratory conditions birds, like humans, do not always behave entirely naturally.

Reptiles, tortoises, snakes and iguana never dream although they spend 60 per cent of their time asleep. Crocodiles, it is said, dream considerably more than birds. All mammals, on the other hand, dream and can be divided into two distinct groups – the hunter and the hunted. The hunters, and those include dogs, cats, ferrets and man, all dream for 20 to 25 per cent of their sleep-time. The hunted, which include cattle, deer, goats, sheep and rabbits, sleep less anyway but most of this is non-dreaming sleep. Only 6 to 8 per cent of their sleep is spent in REM dreaming. And who can blame them? To survive they have to keep very much in touch with reality so dreaming about symbolic, pie-in-the-sky abstractions associated with REM sleep would be of secondary importance to them!

Sleep
Before we can dream we have to sleep and each night we slip off into an unconscious state that could be frightening if we were not so familiar with it. Usually this is very welcome especially after a tiring day and it is, perhaps, a state similar to that long sleep of death. Experiences during sleep are certainly akin to those brought back by people who have died clinically, but this is another story.

Until this century the only clue we had about sleep came from our remembered dreams but with electronic monitoring of brain waves all this changed. Before this technique was developed it was impossible to investigate sleep for the simple reason that we could not study it without disturbing it. This can be compared with bird-watching before binoculars were invented; approach them and the birds, like sleep, flew away.

The Purpose of Sleep
The Common Sense theorists originally believed that the purpose of sleep was to allow us to rest physically. This belief was soon shattered when it was found that if a person was allowed to lie down and rest for twenty-four hours but kept awake for this time, he was restored physically but exhausted if not deranged mentally. In a series of time-lapsed photographs taken during sleep the body was seen to make continual efforts to prevent too much physical

relaxation and in one night alone it is normal to turn over up to twenty times. This is in order to actually exercise our muscles. At this point the Common Sense adherents changed their minds and said it was not really physical rest we needed during sleep at all, it was mental rest.

Turning their attention to the brain, the most important organ in our body, it seemed reasonable to assume that this could well be the case. Our brain is, after all, working away all day thinking, reasoning and remembering, so surely it deserved rest. Unfortunately, this assumption had to go too because the very evidence intended to remove once and for all any mystery attached to sleeping and dreaming, clearly revealed that the brain was just as active during sleep as it was when we were awake.

On examining biofeedback data received from brain monitoring, early researchers soon realized that although impulses altered from a fast, low amplitude when awake, to a slow, high amplitude when asleep, there was no evidence whatsoever to suggest any decrease in the brain's activity. If anything, there was more and it was this that finally wrecked their belief that dreams were physical in origin and pathological.

To them, the most important aspect of sleep had been that it should be completely undisturbed and dreamless, so if dreams interfered with this then it followed that they must be abnormal. Today, we know the reverse of this to be true. If sleep is inadequate, either in quantity or quality, dreams do not manifest as they should and the result of this is mental confusion.

What is Sleep?

In attempting to understand sleep and the brain, they have been compared with many things, including radio broadcasting, the telephone, television and now the computer. Using computer language researchers say we are 'on-line' for two-thirds of a day and 'off-line' for the other third. When we are 'off-line' during sleep our brain, like that of a computer, is not idle or resting but is busy reassessing, classifying and updating the day's input. It then abandons all irrelevant outdated information. Our dreams, according to these theorists, are like the siftings from this abandoning process.

Even assuming this analogy to be correct it is still only a fragment of the whole concept of sleep and we shall need a lot more than man-made electronic gadgets to discover the real truth. It is, however, true that we often wake in the morning and find our problems have lessened and even been solved and we sometimes come up with original ideas too, all due perhaps to mental reassessment, computer-fashion. Past memories, however, are not obliterated as in the case of the computer clearance system. They are retained forever. Sleep is, among other things, undoubtedly a great restorative although not in the way earlier researchers once thought. Energy accumulated during sleep is on a different level from energy stored from food and that acquired from physical rest; it has the power to heal us both physically and mentally.

Physical Changes During Sleep

To give the Common Sense theorists their due, many things do happen to us physically as well as mentally when we are asleep and what is more, these changes are undoubtedly responsible for some of our dreams, nightmares and experiences during sleep. Take, for example, that feeling of suddenly stepping off a kerb, the shock of which wakes us with a start. This happens in the early stages of sleep and is due to a reflex action which produces sudden muscular contraction. This is called a myoclonic jerk. The sensation of falling, not to be confused with a dream of flying and weightlessness, also happens in early light sleep and arises from our mental appreciation of that twilight stage between waking and sleeping.

Another sleep experience which is physical in origin is that of seeing a flash of brilliant light, hearing a shot or sensing something like an explosion inside the head. All these are thought to result from electrical stimulation of the occipital region of the brain, in turn due to a build-up of static electricity accumulated in the larger muscles, mainly the limbs. This is then discharged in the form of a self-induced electric shock from the body to the head. As startling as this surge of energy is, it has been known to have beneficial healing effects and is apparently responsible for some remarkable cures.

Paralysis

Paralysis is an unpleasant sensation we sometimes experience in sleep and this is not a dream, nor is it imagination. It is very real indeed. The reason for this is that during sleep the muscular reflexes associated with our limbs completely disappear with the result that we are literally unable to move. When this is incorporated into a dream, as it often is, it is usually one where we are being chased but cannot move! Since the REM sleep state precedes waking, it occasionally happens that this paralysis temporarily overlaps into the awake state, but it goes immediately we open our eyes. Fortunately, involuntary muscular movements associated with our heartbeat and breathing are not affected by this paralysis.

Apnea

If you listen to the rhythmic breathing of a young sleeping child you will notice that every now and then he or she stops breathing for several seconds or what seems like an eternity. This temporary cessation is called apnea and is usual in newborn babies and infants. Some adults, however, continue with this habit right on into old age. Premature babies are particularly prone to this and when they are first born and electrically monitored in their incubators, an alarm bell rings every time they stop breathing. All one has to do to start them breathing again is to give them a little prod! The build-up of carbon-dioxide in the blood, which accumulates when not exhaling, usually stimulates the respiratory system back into action but this mechanism, the co-ordination between voluntary and involuntary actions, is not quite fully developed in those born prematurely. Within weeks, however, they catch up and this problem is then overcome.

Outer and Inner Disturbances

Outer and inner stimuli, not sufficient to awaken us immediately, are sometimes incorporated into our dreams. With ingenuity our economical dreaming mind makes full use of external noises as well as internal physical disturbances and weaves them into meaningful dreams which offer messages to be thought out and interpreted on waking. The paralytic experience is one example and although entirely physical in origin, the dream in which it features nevertheless has a specific meaning. Each night we enter the REM sleep state several times and each time we do we are temporarily paralysed yet this experience is used sparingly in dreams. When it is, it is used to convey a distinct warning, symbolizing our inability to escape from some vital issue in life.

This incredible principle of using all available props to illustrate a point is found time and time again in our dreams but for the most part the stimulating extraneous cause remains unrecognized. This is because, in itself, it has no relevance whatsoever, as the following dream so clearly shows. In this, a lady dreamed that her sister was persistently ringing the front doorbell. Eventually she awoke to find that it was not the front doorbell but the telephone that was ringing. Although a real bell awoke her it was the symbolic use of this that was important. Clearly the message from this dream was to remind the dreamer that her sister was arriving that day; this she had completely forgotten until her dream 'rang a bell' to that effect!

When it comes to dreams using inner stimuli we have only to think of the old wives' tale about eating cheese late at night and this giving us nightmares. The truth is that a late night snack, and not only one of cheese, can give some people indigestion. The aggravation of the stomach is then used as a basis for a disturbing but nevertheless warning dream and with good reason. The message from this is clearly telling the dreamer not to eat last thing at night, or else!

When a pain is acute enough it wakes us up so that we can do something about it at once, but if it is milder and goes on for some time, it can become the theme for a healing dream, in which case a remedy will be given.

False Awakenings

One reason for believing that we wake up in the middle of the night and see strange things in the bedroom like green monsters, weird animals and long departed relatives is that we are actually dreaming that we are awake! This is so real that it is hard, if not impossible, to convince ourselves it simply was a dream! There again, what is fantasy and what is fact, anyway? It is not always easy to decide this when we are awake in the middle of the day let alone asleep in the depth of night.

Hypnosis and Sleep Learning

There are certain similarities between hypnosis and sleep; after all, Hypnos is the god of sleep. A good hypnotic subject will respond well to suggestions put to them during sleep and a poor hypnotic subject will not respond well to suggestions given to them in sleep. Apart from this, the two states have little in common. The EEG tracings support this by showing two very different brain-wave patterns for hypnosis and sleep.

Sleep learning is a form of hypnotic suggestion and was very popular in the late 1950s and 1960s when sleep was regarded as a waste of valuable time. Seeing the brain was doing nothing during the night, or so some experts then thought, it might as well occupy itself with something useful like learning a language. Results, however, did not live up to expectations and when the technique was later described as a form of brainwashing, and that it inhibited the natural process of dreaming, it dropped from fashion. Learning, of course, does take place during sleep and in our dreams, but not in the programmed way thought up by educationalists. A further difficulty encountered was that just as we forget our dreams so too do we forget what we have learned in sleep.

Somnambulism

Somnambulism, better known as sleepwalking, is more common in children than in adults and the reason for this is thought to be because they try to put action into their dreams. This applies to sleeptalking, too, but apparently we tend to grow out of these. Lady Macbeth, however, did not! Since research shows that sleepwalking and talking take place in the NREM stages of sleep this explanation may not be entirely correct, for we might not even be dreaming at that stage.

Dreams and Objects

Without a doubt the most common object about which we dream is a house or building. Forty per cent of these dreams concentrate on the whole structure and these vary from a small flat to a rambling mansion or even to an ugly, sprawling factory. Twenty-five per cent are centred around one room which may be a bedroom, kitchen, dining room, lounge, attic, cellar, office or school-room. Fifteen per cent involve stairs and corridors, eleven per cent focus on doors and exits generally and nine per cent highlight windows.

Dreams of streets and gardens followed by dreams of travelling by car, train, bus, horse, bicycle, aeroplane and walking on foot are next in line with UFOs and space journeys as runners-up. Swimming, playing games, watching a play or film and fighting also feature prominently, with men having five times as many hostile dreams as women. Both males and females, however, experience an equal share of sex dreams.

When it comes to dreaming in colour, only twenty-nine per cent of 3000 dreamers thought they did although possibly everyone does and only this percentage remembers or notices it. The memory of colour, like a dream itself, fades quickly on waking. Concerning the time a dream lasts, for years it was believed that they were over in fractions of a second but now it is thought they last for anything from a few seconds to over thirty minutes.

How Much Sleep Do We Need?

Babies begin life by sleeping 75 per cent of a 24-hour day, although this takes some believing, knowing some babies. The reverse of this time-scale often seems nearer the truth in reality. However, when they are asleep they spend most of their time in REM dreaming sleep and this they do even before they are born. The interesting question arises, 'Of what are they dreaming?' If they have no experience of the outer world, how on earth, asked the Common Sense theorists, could they possibly dream of anything, let alone become excited, happy, angry and even extremely amused at such an innocent age? Whilst many baby-smiles are due to wind, that deep-throated chuckle reminiscent of an experienced old man or woman, heard only in the first three weeks of life, is not. Could this be a sign of some merry private joke? And what of those incredibly bad childhood nightmares arising from terrifying thoughts far removed from the security of warm nurseries and all-thoughts far removed from the security of warm nurseries and all-loving parental care? Difficult birth experiences and bad memories from this are no answer. The Common Sense theorists certainly found it hard to explain why a child should be aware and afraid of things not previously encountered in this life. To the reincarnationist, however, there is no such problem.

Turning to adults, according to French sources, they have 7 hours 20 minutes sleep each night on average but this is very much an individual matter. As we grow older we tend to need less sleep. It was also found that men sleep more than women; extroverts sleep more than introverts and fat people sleep more than thin people.

It is impossible to have too much sleep but if prolonged bouts do occur it usually means we are either catching up on lost dreaming and generally recharging ourselves, or we are ill. Most illnesses require extra sleep for it is during this that self-healing takes place and this is why children go to sleep the moment they feel off-colour, irrespective of the time of day. Unfortunately, as adults we cannot always do this although it would save a lot of trouble if we did.

Early To Bed

Sayings like, 'Early to bed and early to rise, make a man healthy, wealthy and wise' and, 'One hour before midnight is worth three after' have more than a grain of truth in them. Thanks to a Common Sense discovery it has been found that 70 per cent of our deepest non-dreaming sleep occurs during the first third of the night. If sleep before midnight is missed then much of the important NREM sleep is lost, too. Since these words of good advice were given in the days when most people worked harder physically and went to bed earlier, they then made good sense. Added to this, in those days they, like the Common Sense theorists, considered dreamless sleep to be the only kind that was beneficial.

Insomnia

We tend to worry too much about not sleeping and although deprivation of this is exhausting, to become anxious only adds to the problems which caused it in the first place. Parental insomnia, that brought on by wakeful children, is temporary and comparatively short-lived but the long-term danger from this is that the memory of a broken sleeping pattern is retained and may return in later years. This could account for the fact that there are more insomniacs among those who have previously brought up a family than those who have not.

Anxiety, and the complete reverse from this, joyous elation, both inhibit sleep. The reason for this is that in each of these states our mind is over-active and will not switch off when day is done. Excitement-triggered insomnia, however, is fleeting like a dream itself but unfortunately that which is caused by worry tends to become chronic and soon turns into a regular nightmare!

Sleeping Tips

If sleep continues to evade us and we begin to suffer as a result during the day then sleeping pills are the lesser of the two evils but in no way do they cure insomnia. Reading in bed is an excellent way to divert and concentrate our thoughts on something other than problems. Making sure our hands and feet are warm helps too and so does the adoption of a breathing pattern similar to that of the breathing rhythm in sleep. By breathing *in to the count of two, and out to the count of three*, we are imitating this rhythm and in so doing invite and pave the way for that oft elusive state!

It is the restless outward seeking of our thoughts churning worries over and over again and still getting nowhere, that creates that vicious circle of perpetual wakefulness. Robbed of sleep, reasoning powers diminish and deteriorate enormously so the sooner we can convince ourselves that staying awake is a waste of valuable time, the better. Visualization, the creation of imaginary scenes in our mind, is an excellent way of inviting sleep. By focusing our thoughts within, where incidentally they need to be if sleep is ever going to take over, we can change our mental state of mind and level of thinking in readiness.

The scene we create can take any form we choose so long as it is completely free from all associations likely to remind us of trouble and strife or recall painful memories. Listening to the sea with the mind's ear and seeing it with the mind's eye is a very relaxing exercise. Another is to create a personal Garden of Eden, filling it with plants, animals and those people we alone choose and invite into our private sanctuary. Each night we can conjure up this secret place and go there peacefully awaiting the arrival of those timeless gods, Hypnos, Morpheus and Hermes who will soon spirit us away to far-off places amid the Land of Dreams.

Head and Heart

Whether we realize it or not we all have the ability to solve our problems in two different ways, on two distinctly different levels of understanding. When we are awake we use our intellect and reasoning powers but when we are asleep our inspiration and symbolic vision takes over. Figuratively, these contributions are from our heads and from our hearts. The power of dreams which provides the inspirational visions works spontaneously so we are, for the most part, unaware of the unique role it has played in helping us. 'Sleep on it' is advice readily given to those faced with difficult decisions and apparently insoluble situations and most of us have experienced the benefit from doing this. Often we have gone to sleep with fears rampaging through our heads yet on waking in the morning find to our intense relief that the cloud has lifted and hope has returned. And this improvement in our affairs, thanks to our dreaming minds, we usually take for granted.

It is, however, the blending of these two aspects, the intellectual and the inspirational, the head and the heart, that gives us not only original answers to ordinary problems, but enables us, if we really want to, to make unique discoveries as well. But to do this we need to remember the famous words of advice Kekule gave to his students: 'Gentlemen, let us first learn to dream'.

The Source

Where do we go for one third of each twenty-four hour day, and why? The Common Sense theorists discovered, no doubt to their disappointment, that in order to rest physically and mentally, we do not necessarily have to sleep. True, some biological processes such as hormone production, cellular replacement and healing take place at night but this might well occur when we are resting anyway, for we are not then using energy in other ways.

Although this might be yet another approach road to the meaning of dreams it does seem that sleep is our prime state of existence for the sleep-state is just as much an experience as the awake-state. One clue leading to this conclusion is the fact that when we are first born into this world we spend virtually all our time asleep, in dreamland. Slowly but surely we then begin to experience more and more, through our five physical senses, in the dimension we call the real world. Eventually, we stay awake for two-thirds of each twenty-four hour day. During sleep, however, we return to our prime state, a state that was interrupted by us being born into a physical body that seeks expression in periods of wakefulness, limited by the 3-dimension field!

This, of course, is the other side of the coin from the Common Sense view which, along with other things, sought to prove that sleep was the great intruder wedged into wakefulness. If, however, we reverse their all-material concept, life takes on a very different meaning and the real world exists not 'out there' but 'in here' inside us. We can then see it as that dimension religions called heaven and C. G. Jung described as the collective unconscious. And in sleep we return and through our dreams commune with the rest of creation. From this source comes our energy and our inspirations too, which in no way could we receive from intellect alone. Above all, we receive encouragement and hope for the future.

Since the end of the 1939-45 war, the pace of life has quickened to such an extent that the one-third of our time spent in the sleep-state and in communication with 'The Source' is not enough to keep us in balance. Our physical output is too much for our psychological or spiritual input so we seek to recharge during the day. Some snatch forty-winks after lunch but to help make up for this almost chronic deficiency, relaxation and meditation have crept into our daytime activities. What we are attempting to do when we participate in these practices is to consciously contact that great divine source and recharge ourselves.

In seeing 'The Source' as our natural heritage, dreams, coincidences, telepathy, ghosts, UFOs and all the thousand and one things that refuse to fit into the neat compartments made by intellectual thinking, limited by the five senses, need no further explanation. In sleep, however, we return to this Land of Dreams and once we recognize it, our lives take on an added dimension. The real world is no longer what it seems; it is 'The Source' that matters for we were there before we were born, we go there when we sleep and we shall return there after we have died. Is this what Shakespeare meant when he wrote: 'To sleep, to sleep, perchance to dream — ay, there's the rub; for in that sleep of death what dream may come when we have shuffled off this mortal coil?'

3

PSYCHOLOGICAL AND PSYCHIC APPROACHES TO DREAMS

For all the sleeping hours clocked up by the human race and the untold millions of dreams experienced over the years it is a sobering thought to realize that we understand dreams less today than our ancestors did two, three or even four thousand years ago. We may think we are covering new ground when we use dreams to solve problems and try to understand ourselves through them but nothing is new really. It was, however, Sigmund Freud, the father of psychiatry, who altered the way people thought about their dreams and themselves by introducing the psychoanalytical approach. In doing this he updated the old concepts and gave them new names but in some ways this added to the confusion for today there are those who still do not know their Id from their Ego!

Scherner
Drawing on ancient traditional methods of dream interpretation nineteenth-century specialists paved the way nicely for Freud by providing clues, if not direct evidence, for his later psychoanalytical conclusions. Scherner in 1861 introduced the idea of decentralization in sleep, a state whereby fantasy dominated and played games with thoughts by transforming them into symbols. An example he gave was how an impression or feeling in a dream could become an object, rather in the way the Bible says, 'the Word became flesh'. As a form of substitution, the body in a dream was represented by

a house, the lungs were windmills, the heart a clock, the penis a flute and the vagina a cave.

Strupell, Maury, Stricker, Delage and Radestock
In 1877 Strupell authoritatively stated that those who dreamed turned their backs on the world, meaning that dreams were simply escape mechanisms. He also said that stimuli awakened thoughts which materialized visually in dreams and progressed along a chain of ideas. From this, originally called the Law of Association, the famous Freudian Association of Ideas was born. Maury, in 1878, said dreams were repressed intuition and Stricker in 1879 added that one person in five was afraid of robbers in dreams. The robbers were imaginary but their fears were real. He also said that the function of a dream was to be compared with the function of the bowels and bladder; they were, therefore, to be seen as mental processes for eliminating useless thoughts. Delage, also in 1879, saw repressed impressions forming subjects for dreams and at the same time Radestock was busy describing dream images as signs of wish fulfilment. Childhood memories laced with fear, sexual desires, disappointment, substitution, symbolization and the complexes were all out in the open by the latter half of the nineteenth-century but it took Freud to unite them under one big psychological banner.

Sigmund Freud 1856-1939
Professor Sigmund Freud certainly did not believe dreams to be ramblings from uncontrolled minds but saw them as scenes from an unconscious state underlying conscious awareness. Originally he thought they were reflections relating to conscious experiences since he recognized in them symptoms of hysteria, abnormal behaviour and even physical disease, projected symbolically. Hysteria, an abnormal behaviour pattern, and physical symptoms are symbolic in themselves anyway since they are secondary effects from a primary cause. For example, a rash is a physical effect but at the same time a symbol reflecting its underlying cause; and on a mental level the person who vomits easily may not be able to digest unpalatable facts so this, in turn, symbolizes the cause.

By encouraging his patients to go on talking at length about their dreams and the off-theme thoughts they provoked, Freud perfected his chain reaction technique now popularly known as the Free Association of Ideas. However irrational the ideas were, avoidance of the truth seemed to Freud to be apparent by its absence. From this came his theory of repression and wish fulfilment. After formulating the association of ideas Freud tracked down what he called Habitual Complexes, later described by Jung as 'those tender spots of the psyche which react most to stimulus or disturbance'. These complexes are walled-up innermost secrets which we now know can be reached and freed by methods other than through the free association of ideas in dreams. The inkblot test devised by Rorschach serves as an excellent stimulus for this as indeed does any irregular shape or object and in this lies the secret of crystal gazing and scrying. Leonardo da Vinci, incidentally, recognized this chain reaction when he wrote, 'It should not be hard for you to stop sometimes and look into the stains on the wall or the ashes in the fire or the clouds in the sky or even mud, in which you will find really marvellous ideas.'

Freud went to great lengths to maintain his theory that all dreams represented a wish fulfilment. 'The fulfilment of a wish is its only purpose and even dreams with painful contents are to be analysed as fulfilment wishes,' he urged. One difficulty, however, was for him to satisfactorily explain fear and anxiety in wish-fulfilment terms.

Often called the Viennese sexologist, the professor also noticed 'day residues' in dreams which were all mixed up with memories. This observation along with results he achieved with hysterics under hypnosis eventually led him to the development of and treatment through psychoanalysis. By 1893 he expressed his conclusions, declaring that extreme physical symptoms recognized in hysteria were caused not by pathological changes but by emotional psychic energy. This was converted into physical symptoms so that the nervous condition became the 'conversion neurosis'. Later, he described this psychic energy as being sexual in nature and his work with dreams convinced him that all the symbols found in these were projections from repressed sexual hang-ups, laced with guilt.

Ego, Id and Super-Ego

Somewhere along the psychoanalytical trail Freud saw man as a three-part being with three psychological aspects he called the Ego, Id and Super-Ego. In some ways they relate to the present day notion of the Body, Mind and Spirit with the Ego reflecting the conscious more physical self, the Id associated with the mind and its primitive instincts and the Super-Ego in contact with the spirit, higher self and conscience. What Freud thought happened was that during sleep the Ego was absent and the Id, reminiscent of Plato's wild beast, took over with its dominance of basic energy. This manifested as sexual urges and self-preservation which in turn presented as forms of aggression. To protect the Ego and the Super-Ego from such blatant sexual desires the Id did a camouflage job by producing fantastic symbolic dreams in the hope of avoiding a shock. The nineteenth century false modesty and humbug of guilt-ridden Britain was also rife in Europe so this code made a lot of sense at the time. In the light of present-day thoughts on sex, however, it now seems ridiculous, but Freudian psychology does work for some and the free association of ideas can lead to critical hidden fears being revealed. but as the Common Sense theorists soon discovered, there is more than one approach to dreams, and even more roads leading from them.

Carl Gustav Jung 1875-1961

Carl Gustav Jung was Freud's pupil. Although he disagreed with Freud's belief that sexual repression was the underlying stimulating cause of dreams, Jung actually parted company with Freud's theories before this stage, as he states in *Man and His Symbols*:

> Freud attached particular importance to dreams as the point of departure for a process of free association. But after a time I began to feel that this was a misleading and inadequate use of the rich fantasies that the unconscious produces in sleep. My doubts really began when a colleague told me of an experience he had during the course of a long train journey in Russia. Though he did not know the language and could not even decipher the Cyrillic script, he found himself musing over the strange letters and he fell into a reverie in which he imagined all sorts of meanings for them. One idea led to another and

in his relaxed state he found that this free association had stirred up many old memories. This episode opened my eyes to the fact that it was not necessary to use a dream as the point of departure for the process of free association.

This shows that Jung had his own ideas about dreams early on, believing they had a special purpose of their own which indicated an underlying idea or intention which was not apparent on the surface. He began, therefore, to pay attention to the actual form of a dream rather than fly off at a tangent on the free association of ideas trail. This technique was diametrically opposed to Freud's free association for it was intended to exclude, not encourage, irrelevant thoughts which could, no doubt, lead to complexes but Jung, like the soothsayers of old, recognized in dreams powers well beyond personal neurotic traits. You could say that his catch phrase in this respect was, 'Yes! But let us get back to the dream, not away from it.'

The Anima and Animus

Jung researched ancient beliefs and dreams extensively and found that the pattern of the universe was one of duality and this quality existed within individuals as well as in nature. It was not, he found, only on the physical level where physiology demonstrated it as male and female hormones present in both sexes, but on psychic levels too. The feminine element in the male character Jung called anima and the masculine element in the female character he called the animus. From this division of the personality came the notion that the unconscious self was very different from the conscious self and Jung described the following dream to illustrate his point. A man dreamed of a dishevelled, vulgar woman who seemed to be his wife although in reality his wife was not like this at all. On the surface the dream was unacceptable so was rejected as nonsense but when Jung applied his duality theory the man's anima entered the scene, meaning that the feminine compassionate side of his nature was neglected. This showed he was behaving like a degenerate female of whom better things were expected. Conversely, the woman who dreamed of a knight in shining armour would, in Jungian terms, be reflecting the gallant, positive side of herself.

Throughout life we undergo a process of what Jung called individuation whereby the two aspects of the self, the anima and the animus, the feminine and the masculine, attempt to unite. Eventually this would lead to the mystical marriage Jung mentions, but since few recognize the purpose of dreams on the practical level let alone the psychic, this experience, he said, is rare.

Signs, Symbols, Archetypes and the Collective Unconscious

If signs and symbols are not Jungian in origin, archetypes and the collective unconscious certainly are. The definition Jung gave to signs, symbols and archetypes are, however, unique and to quote his words, they are as follows: 'The sign is always less than the concept it represents while the symbol always stands for something more than its obvious and immediate meaning. Archaic remnants I call Archetypes or primordial images.'

In practice a trademark is a sign for something else and since the comparison is invented it can never be a symbol in its own right. A symbol, on the other hand, hints at something not yet known and it is this that occurs spontaneously in dreams. Symbols happen, they are not inventions of the conscious mind and as such are our main source of knowledge in this respect, occurring in dreams, daydreams, visions and psychic phenomena.

Archetypes appear in dreams, daydreams, visions and phenomena too, again without the dreamer having prior knowledge of their existence but whereas an archetype is a symbol, a symbol is not necessarily an archetype. One explanation for archetypes in dreams is that primordial images form part of an inherited ancestral memory. Just as we inherit physical characteristics going back to primitive biological life-patterns, so too do we possess primary mental essences arising from a collective psyche. An archetype is not, therefore, a mythological image although it is often mistaken and represented as such; the mythological image is, in turn, a symbol for an underlying force. In this lies the mystery and meaning of the ancient gods, each of whom symbolized and represented a different force and principle of nature and the universe.

The source from which all this stemmed Jung called the collective unconscious but, again, this was not an entirely new concept. As he himself said, 'It is the foundation of what the ancients called the sympathy of all things.' Others might equally well call it the Akashic records but whatever name we give it, it does seem that from this universal reservoir there flows a stream of powerful cosmic memories which we contact, or perhaps they contact us, through our dreams.

It is not easy to compare the Freudian Id, Ego and Super-Ego with the Jungian Unconscious, Conscious and the Collective Unconscious although there does seem to be a relationship so far as levels of awareness go. Their contents, however, are very different. The Freudian Id, for example, like the Jungian Unconscious, is a sub-region of the mind. But the Id is more a repository bulging with sexual repressions whereas the Jungian Unconscious contains the anima and animus, the dual aspects or complementary halves of the self. The main difference between a Freudian and Jungian approach to dreams, however, is best recognized in the difference in the treatment the same dream would receive.

If the main symbol in a dream was, say, an apple then the leading off on the Freudian free association of ideas trail would go like this: 'Apple, pears, stairs, bedroom, bed and sex.' Alternatively, the Jungian treatment of the apple symbol would be more like this: 'Apple, knowledge, wisdom, but what about the apple? Apple, food for thought. Apple, tree of life, family tree, family problems. Back again to the apple; temptation in the Garden of Eden.' By applying the meanings directly associated with the symbol the underlying meaning would eventually be revealed. Jung also favoured a series of dreams, associating one with the next to unravel his patients' problems whereas Freud concentrated on one at a time as isolated incidents.

Alfred Adler 1870-1937
Alfred Adler did not accept the concept of the unconscious in the way Freud and Jung did, so it is not surprising that he saw dreams as little more than exaggerated forms of wishful-thinking day-dreams. That he saw dreams as wish fulfilments is certain although

he did not use this term nor did he see sex as an underlying theme as did Freud. By concentrating on Freud's habitual complexes, however, Adler isolated one of these and then divided it into two, giving us the ever-popular superiority and inferiority complexes. These terms originated from observing what he called 'Organ inferiority'. This was a physical defect or deformity leading to over-compensation of the personality.

As an example of this he gave that of the Kaiser with his paralysed arm. He made up for this inadequacy, said Adler, by developing a power-hungry craze to rule the world. Another example was small men who often became dominant in society due to their effort to comply with a driving compensation complex but if a goal was too far removed from reality and they failed in their attempt to reach it they became victims of a nervous breakdown, making excuses like, 'If only I had not had the 'flu I would easily have succeeded.' This lament was typical of those who over-compensated and allowed their superiority to lead them astray. None of this is manifested in dreams though, according to Adler.

The Adlerian urge to power was exclusively masculine in character although if one accepts the Jungian concept of the anima and especially the animus it can be seen as a driving force in women too. We can also see how the Walter Mitty day-dream was hard for Adler to distinguish from the wish fulfilment night-dream but he did just about recognize that occasionally dreams symbolically reflected the personal battle between the inferiority and superiority complexes of the self.

With Freud's psychoanalysis, Jung's analytical psychology and Adler's individual psychology it is clear to see from whence the present-day forms of psychology and social psychotherapy sprang. So far as dreams are concerned the psychological approach is more interested in their investigation than in their interpretation although the two aspects are closely connected and in a way inseparable, but what is new on the psycho-psychic dream front? One type of dream does seem to have been sadly neglected by the three pioneers and this is the dream in which we know we are dreaming, called a lucid dream. Freud mentions this type only briefly in the later editions of his work when he agreed that consciousness could enter into a dream whereby the dreamer would know if he or she were dreaming but to comply with his wish-fulfilment theory and remain ever true to himself he added that this was 'due to the wish to enjoy the dream to the full'.

The Psychic Approach

The dreamers of old who attributed their nightly experiences to external forces took the psychic approach to dreams. Undoubtedly, they believed God and His angels, the gods and goddesses of nature, various spirits and the discarnate entities who helped them were at man's disposal and could be contacted through dreams when necessary. In those days they deliberately invoked these influences by incubating their dreams but even without doing this, psychic dreams can and do occur spontaneously. When they do they are usually recognized as great spiritual truths and enlightening experiences which have the power to alter a destiny, solve a problem or heal physically or mentally. Unfortunately, there are also other external influences and forces around which are far from beneficial, nor are they benevolent, and it is these that are terrifying nightmares known as psychic or incubus attacks. Children are far more susceptible to these than adults and whilst not all nightmares are psychic in origin, it seems that some are.

Psychic attacks via dreams are more likely when we are ill, particularly if we have a fever and the possible reason for this is that our aura, that protective energy-field around us, is weakened to the extent that it is easily breached. It is this aspect of dreaming that leads us into the parapsychological field where there is still much to be explained. Telepathy, prophecy, astral travelling and communication with those long dead are possible, as evidence shows, but the ultimate goal, if one is to work in this field of experience, must surely be in the understanding of lucid dreams, where we have a degree of control over them.

Lucid Dreams

Since the 1960s and the mushrooming of psychic and religious groups there has been an interest in what are called enlightening dreams. These include lucid dreams. Unless a dream is full of prophecy, magical symbols and plenty of astral projection members of these groups consider it to be valueless. This is because they do not seem to know that dreams reflect life as a whole, from the ordinary to the extraordinary. To single out any one aspect of dreaming, psychic or otherwise, presupposes that one facet of life is more important than another which, of course, it is not.

Recent interest in the beliefs of the mystic Mexican, Don Juan via Carlos Castaneda, exemplifies the present emphasis on psychic dreams for Don Juan saw them as aids to the development of psychic and mental powers. To increase these powers, he said, one had to become conscious whilst dreaming and then learn how to manipulate the dream. This brings us back to lucid dreaming which until recently was thought to be so rare and unimportant that Freud, Jung and Adler virtually ignored it. When, however, a group of average people, not selected dreamers with an interest in dreams, were asked if they ever had a dream in which they knew they were dreaming, 73 per cent said they had. This shows that lucid dreams are far more frequent than the experts previously thought and their importance lies in the fact that they form a link between psychological, psychic and mystical aspects of the mind and the universe, too.

van Eeden and Dr Keith Hearne

The term 'lucid dreaming' was first used at the beginning of this century by a Dutchman named van Eeden, himself a prolific lucid dreamer. Sometimes he found that these dreams were preceded two or three nights before with flying dreams but the main distinguishing feature of a lucid dream is that we know, without a shadow of a doubt, that we are dreaming. The scene is very real in one sense but from personal experience I find the improbable and the impossible are sometimes there too, although at the time it does not seem to be a bit out of place or odd.

Dr Keith Hearne from Hull has made an extensive study of lucid dreams. In his dream laboratory, he has instigated a new method of ocular signalling which establishes communication between the sleeping subject and the dream investigator. Another aspect of his work is directed towards encouraging lucid dreams by producing an external stimulus from a special apparatus called 'a dream machine'. Apart from discovering further electro-physiological information which shows the type of sleep and brain-waves associated with lucid dreaming, Dr Hearne has also found that these dreams have both psychological and psychic implications far beyond those recognized in dreams generally by Freud and Jung. It seems that once we acknowledge the possibility of dreaming lucidly, they respond and although it is still early days his latest inroad in this direction could prove to be the most important and revealing yet.

Within the bounds of lucid dreams there are many aspects of awareness. In one we may find ourselves saying, 'This is ridiculous. It can't possibly happen so I must be dreaming.' You could say this is the analytical way of looking at a dream when actually dreaming, the counterpart of which is that waking experience where, when something nasty happens, we say hopefully, 'I don't believe it. I will wake up in a minute and find it is a ghastly dream.' In lucid nightmares we do wake up but unfortunately there is no such escape from the daytime experience!

Apart from this conscious rationalization during a dream this awareness or lucidity can have psychic association too, but unless the dreamer recognizes and understands this the experience is simply filed away and forgotten among, no doubt, other valuable but wasted dreams. It is, therefore, no understatement to say that the latent potential in a lucid dream is enormous but the secret of releasing this potential lies in being able to control the dream itself. If we can do this then we can begin to control our own lives and we may even be able to alter our course of destiny, if necessary. This introduces the question of free will, which most of us believe we have, at least to some degree.

The Control of Dreams

The next stage beyond that of knowing we are dreaming is when we begin to control and manipulate a dream and make things happen that we want to happen. Just as we can control and create day-dream images, so too can we control and create a dream when asleep, but there are important distinctions between the two. During sleep our awareness is far more acute than when awake. On a scientific level this is registered as altered brain-wave patterns and in practice it manifests itself as prophetic warnings and messages, healing, flashes of enlightenment and the ability to achieve feats well beyond our wildest dreams.

Since it is possible to control a lucid dream and since there is a relationship between lucid dreaming and future events, the implications are enormous. This, of course, is why those psychic groups are so fascinated with lucid dreams, but quite apart from a specialized interest like this there is no reason why any one of us cannot use dreams in this way to help us along the often stony road through life. Problem solving and self-healing as well as many other personal goals are well within our scope if we really want to make use of our incredible dream power.

The Cause of Dreams

The inevitable question is, who or what initiates, designs and even decides that we need a particular dream, on a certain night, in the first place? In other words, what is the cause of dreams? Since appropriate dreams always come at the right time and even before time when they are prophetic, chance can be ruled right out. The Common Sense theorists are content with their biological explanation of a physical cause, the psychologists remain satisfied with underlying psychological reasons and the psychics are happy in their conviction that discarnate beings and strange forces are responsible, so where are we? The multiple choice of dream-producing stimuli coming from without, from within, from above and from who knows where else is most unsatisfactory, especially since all are so plausible in their own right. If, however, we take into account the law of cause and effect on a grand scale it is possible to see that none of these are explanations at all, nor are they causes in themselves. They are all effects.

From this standpoint it is clear to see why the Common Sense theory makes sense. But what is seen as a cause, say indigestion, is in fact only an effect with the ensuing nightmare reflecting symbolically the symptoms and sufferings of an overstuffed stomach. By regressing this one stage the reason for the gorging is found. A celebration dinner, arranged perhaps months ago, and from here the trail leads back and back in time, events and associations until eventually childhood, babyhood and maybe even a time before that is reached. In this light the dream is no longer seen as the direct result of a physical cause; it is now simply an effect in a much longer chain of action and reaction. And psychological dreams conform in exactly the same way, showing, for example, the Freudian sexual cause to be nothing more than an effect, like a bead on the thread of life. No hang-up, sexual or otherwise, is ever an isolated cause in itself, in or out of a dream, for that matter.

Prophetic dreams where a scene clearly shows future events appear to prove the exception to this rule but they too fit into this pattern. It is not the succession of cause and effect that has altered but our appreciation and perception of time which has. This is because we are conditioned to consciously perceive time only in chronological order but time has another unconscious concept which has little or no place in our restricted three-dimensional world, so, in our waking state, it is suppressed. When it does get a look-in, however, we call it coincidence.

The ancients knew all about time in both these contexts and called them Chronos and Cairos, to describe the difference between experiencing time (Chronos) and the appreciation of the quality of time (Cairos). Chronos is measured in seconds, minutes, days, years and centuries, thus giving us experiences in chronological order as we travel along life's highway. Alternatively, Cairos, its name, incidentally, showing its link with ancient Egypt, is actual participation within time itself, giving us those out-of-time, timeless moments. It is during Cairos that synchronistic events occur which we call coincidences. Once we become aware of time in these ways, prophetic experiences in dreams need no further explanation for past, present and future all exist and belong to the eternal now.

Returning to the ultimate cause of a dream, it seems to me that no single cause or stimulus can, therefore, possibly be isolated, other than that of ourselves. Experiences, influences, inheritances, environment, temperament, parents and ancestors all contribute to our individual destiny and dreams, like mirrors, reflect all this – and more! Every dream event is linked in a different way, if we could but see it, so there is no cause as such, only effects. And if we could fully understand this linking pattern, we would discover not only the secret of dreaming but the secret of life itself. This, however, is a dream of the future, for the future.

4

DREAMS AND THEIR SCHEMES

Dream interpreters of old were interested only in dreams and their meanings, not the dreamer and his or her state of mind. Joseph, for example, did not want to know about Pharaoh's psychological problems any more than Daniel wondered what indigestible food Nebuchadnezzar had eaten for his supper to cause his dream. It was their dream messages that mattered and when all is said and done, this is what dreaming is all about.

A dream interpreter is a dream analyst working entirely with dreams. A psychoanalyst, on the other hand, is interested in the dreamer's state of mind and works secondarily with his dreams in order to understand that person. As a dream analyst, I do not discuss dreams with the dreamer and if I did it would, from my standpoint, amount to cheating! After all, by looking at a person and asking a few pertinent questions it is easy to learn all you need to know about him and his dream! It is, however, the dream that needs analysing, not the dreamer, so if one has a preconceived idea about the dreamer this obviously colours and distorts the whole interpretation. Many letters I receive describing dreams are signed with initials only so they might well be from a man or a woman but this in no way alters the interpretation. Why should it?

Messages From Ourselves To Ourselves
Having interpreted over 12,000 dreams I must confess to having

paved yet another approach road to dreams. This one focuses attention completely on the dream itself, without knowledge or help from the dreamer. When searching for a reliable foundation upon which to build an interpretational framework it seemed important that the first step should be to lay down concrete definitions, where possible. Obviously, dreams are messages but as we see from history, literature, religions and scientific investigations, no one is sure who sends them. Having considered this without much success the answer came, not surprisingly, from a dream. In this I was looking and talking to myself in a mirror! On waking and on reflection, it was abundantly clear that dreams were indeed messages, but from no one else other than ourselves. The more I looked at them this way the more sure I was that they were unique creations which sometimes seemed to have been triggered off by inner and outer stimuli which were incorporated into our dreams, but we were still the originators. The first definition had, therefore, to be that dreams were messages from ourselves to ourselves. From the psychological standpoint there are no holds barred when messages of self-truths are revealed in a dream, for the barrier between conscious and unconscious levels is down. This explains how all those repressed urges, fears and long-lost memories come to light so effortlessly, but to limit dreams to the role of psychological policeman only is to under-estimate them completely, for this is only one facet, important as it is, of many.

The Dreaming Mind

To bridge the gap between the conscious and unconscious minds there had to be something to help convey thoughts and the dream across so, for a second definition and want of a better one, I called it The Dreaming Mind. In a way this is the dream itself but, whatever this link really is, it is there when we are awake as well as when we are asleep. If you think about it, when we mull over past memories or consciously conjure up thoughts for the future, two-way traffic starts up as we mentally pass back and forth between the conscious and unconscious. This bridge also accounts for day-dreaming and those rare but remarkable visions which occur spontaneously and refuse to fit into logical reasoning. Daydreams, visions, psychic phenomena and vivid imaginings, however, are not the same as dreams, although they all share certain characteristics.

Types of Dreams

The next step towards understanding dreams is to try to identify the different types of dreams, but this is not as easy as it sounds. There are so many, from fear dreams, wishful-thinking dreams, sad dreams, sex dreams, to a thousand and one other types of dreams, too. In fact if you add virtually any adjective to the word 'dream' you have another type! Fortunately, two of my dreams came to the rescue at the appropriate time and although neither of them produced startling messages as such, they revealed something other than this.

In the first dream I was busy painting and wallpapering my kitchen, as I had actually done a few weeks before. It was as realistic as if I had actually been there but apart from this nothing else happened. The other dream that same night was completely different. The setting was an unfamiliar house and I was searching in strange rooms for something among old, discarded furniture. It was impossible to describe either of these dreams as frightening, happy, sexy or anything else for that matter, yet they just had to be something! Both were set in houses, one familiar and one not and I was the only person involved in each of them. Eventually, it dawned on me that the first dream was a literal dream and the second was a symbolic dream. Here, then, were not just two types of dreams but two basic differences, or principles. From this it seemed logical to suppose that all dreams were either literal, symbolic or a mixture of the two. Once having recognized this, then and only then, could prefixes like fearful, warning, sexy, psychic or what have you, be added to further identify and label them as various types of dreams.

Literal Dreams

Literal dreams reflect the outside world in a practical, unemotional, and as far as possible, intellectual way. They show literal scenes where problems and solutions can be seen and sorted out logically in the cold light of day, with the head, not the heart. It is not surprising that there is a high literal content in many dreams when we consider that children are taught from an early age to think clearly and without silly imaginings. Once conditioned like this, even the dreaming mind gives in and presents its offerings in the same literal vein.

Some people do not recognize the existence of literal dreams, so consequently try to give symbolic meanings where none are intended. By reading mystery into them they complicate a straightforward dream and so miss the point, not to mention the message, completely. What we have to remember is that there are no symbols in literal dreams, only signs, and these are meant to be taken at face value.

Dogmatic intellectual thinkers tend to have literal, unimaginative dreams because this is the way they think and this is the only possible way they could accept a message from their dreams. This, of course, limits their vision but once the dream-gates of perception are opened their literal dreams soon become interspersed with symbols representing hitherto unknown qualities, potential and originality.

Action-Replay Dreams

Literal dreams then, reflecting and relating to the familiar world about us, faithfully reproduce scenes and people as they really are. They may recall past memories, show present situations and reveal future events but one thing is certain and that is they are never sentimental. Vividly revived childhood events and memories, for example, are not idle fantasies for old times' sake, they are for a very good reason.

Rarely, if ever, do dreams go over the past happenings simply for the heaven or hell of it. Reliving bad events allows the dreamer to see them differently in the hope of being able to accept or come to terms with whatever it is that is relived. If it is frightening or even sad these dream experiences can innoculate mentally against the pain and anguish. On the other side of this coin there are the funny happenings repeated to show that laughter is the best medicine and that life has its lighter side. Passionate moments, too, are welcome action-replays, if only to reinforce or stoke up romantic feelings. The agony and the ecstasy of love dreams are stop-gaps for those who cannot be with the one they love, and if the heart rules exclusively in these, then so much the better!

Literal dreams are action-replays and can be compared with Saturday afternoon sport on television where a re-run of events shows the scoring of a goal, the winning horse or the cricketer caught out. When looking at these action-replay shots for the second time we notice so much more than we did the first time around, and so it is with action-replay dreams.

The purpose of these dreams therefore, is to give us another chance to re-assess a particular incident or situation we did not fully understand at the time. If an experience was misconstrued at the time it had wrong associations from the start so consequently was filed away in the memory in the wrong place. In this we see shades of Freud's association of ideas along with crossed wires and inevitable hang-ups but by dreaming them over again as action-replays, we are given a wonderful opportunity to relive those events, and see them for what they really are. This should enable us to put the record and our memory filing system right!

Warnings and Prophecies

One example showing how this worked in practice came from a lady employed in a large open-plan office. In her dream she was sitting at her desk listening suspiciously to workmates talking and whispering about her. On waking she realized that her dream was an exact action-replay of what had happened the previous day but going over the dream, she discovered that as well as whispering, the women involved in this were huddled together as if looking down at something. Suddenly, the truth dawned on her. It was her birthday next day so could the conspiracy and secrecy possibly concern her birthday card and not her?

As well as showing the dreamer the truth about her paranoic character, this dream also gave her a faithful reproduction of the incident, plus something she had missed the first time around. She now saw it in a very different light, which was just as well, since she had indeed made a mistake the first time. The next day she received a birthday card from the colleagues whom she suspected so unjustly!

Another example of help given by a literal action-replay dream came from a man who dreamed he was driving his car along a familiar road and when he put his foot on the brake nothing happened and he crashed into a wall. He was not hurt but because it was such a realistic dream he felt sure it was a premonition of an impending accident. Interpreting this literally, I had to tell him that first and foremost it was a warning dream about the way he drove and the way he maintained his car, especially in relation to the brakes. He replied saying that his brakes badly needed relining but having done this he was now confident that the dream had been a warning after all, not a prophecy. To this I pointed out that it might well have been prophetic – if he had not heeded the warning it gave!

Both these dreams show just how much more our unconscious minds absorbs compared with our conscious mind and how it then takes the trouble to project this information to us as literal dream warnings. True, under hypnosis similar details can sometimes be recalled but with illuminating dreams like these, appearing at exactly the right time, who needs to bother with that?

Symbolic Dreams

Symbolic dreams arise from the unconscious mind and reflect our inner world of intuition and inspiration. This world is inhabited with feelings, which for the most part cannot be expressed in words. Words like fear, anger, love and hate are merely superficial labels for these feelings and beyond this they cannot be intellectualized further. Experiencing them intuitively, however, is a very different matter and this is where dream symbology fits in for this is to intuition what words are to intellect.

We are not as familiar with our inner world as we are with the outer overshadowing world mainly because right from childhood we are taught to keep a tight rein on feelings and suppress them altogether, if possible. When a child has a tantrum, this is regarded as something of a disgrace yet how else can he express a particular feeling which the most intellectual adult could not put into words, let alone the child who cannot even speak? This is where symbolic dreams fit in. In the case of children their frustrated feelings are freed in sleep and emerge as nightmares;

and their parents unknowingly contribute to the cause of these simply because they do not realize tantrums and dreams are wordless symbolic expressions.

Symbolic dreams, then, reflect feelings and emotions but not all by a long way are concerned with hang-ups and bad experiences which cannot be put into words. Many give birth to intuition, inspirations, messages from God, the gods, an angel or some discarnate spirit. Psychic experiences and universal archetypes are expressed, too. The secret, however, of understanding messages from symbolic dreams is not to replace one symbol with another, as so often happens in psychic circles, for this only takes us further away, not closer, to the meaning. What we have to do is to bring it back into the realm of common sense and reasoning, otherwise it is impossible to ever understand its message.

If we look at dream symbols in much the same way as we look at trademarks it is easy to understand the logic of the heart and the subtle force behind it. The commercial world of hard-sell advertising knows all about symbolism. Their advertising campaigns are based almost entirely on this principle, knowing that subliminal influence pays off handsomely, especially on the financial level! Our everyday outer world is injected with these clever symbolic innuendoes, with every advert appealing first to the heart then to the head and finally to the purse. Yet, as clever as these ploys are and as much petrol we buy because of the tiger it puts in the tank, our dreams are far, far cleverer than this.

It is the translating of dream symbols into reason that causes all the trouble, yet this is not difficult once the different worlds of the intuitive heart and the intellectual head have been recognized. True, they are as different as one of the five senses is from the others and we all know how hard it is to express one of these in terms of another. Try describing a sound in terms of the sense of smell. It is all a question of representational systems, each with their own set of rules and references, yet each is capable of expressing the same thing, differently.

The message from the following dream is an example of this and could easily have been dismissed as illogical ramblings if the dreamer had not been told that it represented an aspect of his own life. In this the dreamer was walking down an unfamiliar road when he reached a dark, miserable hovel. Grey clouds loomed overhead, and he went inside where he found a poor, pathetic creature wearing clothes similar to those his wife wore. He did not recognize this person and felt sorry for her.

In essence this is all there was to the dream and on waking the misery and gloom weighed heavily on him all day. Having used a stand-in for his wife and substituted his familiar home with a dismal scene on the road to nowhere his dreaming mind had done a good symbolic job on his existing domestic scene. The message from this, which came easily once it was applied to his own circumstances, showed all too clearly how dismal his homelife was and how he really did not know his own wife.

The Head and the Heart

We spend our time, even though we do not notice it, letting our heads and our hearts take turns in ruling. There are, of course, those who always let their heads rule their hearts and vice versa, producing characters who are either too earthbound for words or too far from reality and never do come down to earth. The literal head and the symbolic heart also have their say in dreams and the way we think and react as individuals, and the nature of the problem in particular, are factors which help decide if the dream is to be literal, symbolic, or a mixture of the two. This, of course, is an over-simplification of a complex subject and does not bear too close an inspection. To begin with, even the most literal dreams use stand-ins and whilst these are not symbols, they are recognizable signs such as objects or people, representing something or someone else. An example of this is a dream many people have featuring a policeman. The scene is literal, right down to the buttons on the policeman's uniform but this policeman is acting out a special dream role to highlight either authority, arbitration, law and order or even guilt and fear, depending on the dreamer's experiences and associations, so far as the police are concerned.

Dreams and Practical Problems

Sometimes, the head and the heart, intelligence and intuition, do battle with a result that they blow a fuse and produce a void not unlike the rapid transit system of those so-called black holes in space! Some might call this a brainstorm, a real nightmare,but whatever it is we still have to come down to earth and put such dream messages into action if we want to solve our problems. Problems are basically intellectual or psychological but it does not follow that literal dreams necessarily represent practical problems and symbolic dreams represent psychological, heart-felt problems. Many tunes are being played at the same time!

Practical dreams, however, tend to reflect everyday problems associated with the home, work, careers and all academic subjects. The realm of the head rules during the day mostly but with a bit of luck the heart has its say at night so again these dreams may be either symbolic, literal or a bit of both. One of the most profound examples of this was when Professor Kekule dreamed up the symbolic solution to his practical chemical problem and so discovered the elusive benzine ring theory.

Less profoundly, one of my dreams helped me in a similar way. When first teaching relaxation I knew I needed a special piece of music to help with this but gave up the search because none seemed to be what I was looking for. As soon as I stopped looking and listening outwardly it was as if I gave my dreaming mind a chance because right away I dreamed of the music of a popular Cha-Cha, the name of which I never did find out. Instead of the usual quick tempo though, it was played in the dream in a very slow four-four rhythm, rather in the style of the hymn 'O God our Help in Ages Past'. This did not mean anything at all to me until several weeks later when I read how research with music showed that the breathing rate, blood-pressure, heartbeat and brain waves all slowed down to keep in tune and in time with music that had four-four time, namely, sixty beats to the minute. This was the music I needed. It could be anything just so long as it was played slowly as a largo! Every time I hear that popular Cha-Cha now I want to hear it in that slow time but the only time I ever did was in my dream.

Psychological Dreams
Psychological dreams reflect inner personal problems like private

thoughts, feelings, hopes, failures, fears, loves and all the secrets of the heart. These can be safely exposed in dreams without the fear of prying eyes and the passing of judgment from others. When crossed wires fuse and the memory filing system is disorganized a psychological dream is then very useful in dredging up that which needs bringing to the surface. Often, the most helpful of these dreams are the nastiest but when it is remembered that they are reflecting bad memories and poor situations anyway this is exactly as they should be. Life is not a bed of roses so why should dreams reflect anything other than the truth, which is just what this next dream did for a distressed lady.

In her dream she was in a wood, out-numbered by those who wanted to kill her. She felt she had to retaliate and kill them first but when she was faced with the task of actually doing it she could not. This was because her assailants appeared to be pregnant, innocent-looking women who were not as fierce as they at first seemed. The uncomplicated interpretation of this dream shows a desire to commit psychological suicide because of being unable to face up to the situation symbolized by the dream. At the same time she knew for a fact that there were those who actually did wish her harm, probably as a result of something she had done, or not done, in the past. Retaliation, on her part, her dream showed, would be most unfair in the circumstances but the good sign was the pregnant women meant that they, as well as the dreamer, would survive and come out of the wood with new hope for the future.

I later discovered that this dreamer's life was in a state of chaos following traumatic divorce proceedings where she was the so-called guilty party. By applying a bland interpretation to the circumstances only she knew, she was able to see her situation for what it was and above all take comfort in the message that pregnant women symbolized a promise for the future. This, then, was a clarifying and sustaining dream which should have helped her to keep going until she was out of that particularly nasty wood!

When selecting psychological dreams to best illustrate their powers it is difficult to choose any one as being more important than another since all are unique in their own way, but I suppose a dream that alters a person's life for the better, through him or her acting upon its message, is the one that matters most. Just such a dream came from a lady who wrote from a psychiatric ward where she had voluntarily placed herself. In the dream she found herself trapped in a cave and although this did not frighten her unduly she knew she could not find her way out. Suddenly, a strange old woman appeared and quietly said, 'I can show you the way out.' After prodding with her stick the old woman began making a hole in the rock until eventually it was big enough to allow the dreamer to escape into the daylight.

The message from this was so symbolically explicit it seemed a pity to desecrate it by putting it into harsh, inadequate words, but it had to be done if the dreamer was to accept and act consciously upon its message. Obviously, the cave represented the dreamer's unconscious mind which had actually trapped her into believing it was safer to dwell in there than in the conscious outside world. It symbolized a sanctuary for her which she equated in reality with the security of the hospital ward. The old woman was the wise old woman within the dreamer who had the power not only to get her out of her depression but liberate her from herself. The most important part of this message, however, was to show that she must and could rely on herself in the future, which is what she did and has done ever since the dream.

The Language of Dreams

When it comes to the language of dreams our dreaming mind does not limit itself in any way, extravagantly using all sorts of signs, symbols and words. Nor does it keep to one language, either, for the odd foreign phrase is often thrown in for good measure just as a sprinkling of spice is added to the stew. But this is to be expected because in so doing dreams are reflecting exactly what we do when awake anyway. We all talk a lot to get our message over and the conversation we use is made up of remarkable comparisons, puns and proverbs, so why should our dreams not follow suit? 'Out of the frying pan and into the fire' describes some situations perfectly so imagine what scope this sort of talk gives to the dreaming mind when composing it into a dream. The transformation of a situation into a dream, incidentally, is very similar to that of a book being made into a film but the

unique thing about this is that the dreamer not only wrote it, but
was also screen director, stage manager, actor, actress and the
viewing audience all rolled into one. If that is not pure magic then
I do not know what is!

Shapes and Colours

The basic language of dreams, as well as that of the unconscious, is
one of shapes and colours. The first toys given to a baby, furry
animals apart, are strange sets of coloured shapes. We see rows of
bright beads strung across prams and in cots lie assortments of red,
yellow, green, blue and pink circles, triangles, squares, oblongs
and ovals in various combinations and sizes to form what are oddly
called rattles. The baby did not choose them but manufacturers
and adults whose unconscious minds know all about the basic
language of the mind, although if you asked them, would deny all
knowledge of it, did. In fact grown-ups enjoy playing with these
coloured shapes more than a baby because this links them with that
collective, fundamental world of shape and colour.

When a baby leaves the coloured shapes behind they may be
forgotten consciously but never unconsciously. Every single
object they see in life from then on will be compared progressively
with these colours and shapes for these are the basic terms of
reference for the outer world. Things, henceforth, will be
described as round, square, triangular, oblong or oval and
although this simplicity is superceded by complicated and
conventional objects and the distinct contrast in colours loses its
brightness, the original shapes and colours are still retained in the
memory. And for good reason.

When distinct coloured shapes appear in dreams they often
symbolize conditions relating to health. Just as there are over one
hundred adjectives to describe pain, so too are there countless
shapes to represent various complaints and conditions. In self-
healing techniques using conscious imagery and visualization,
every symptom, fear or pain is transformed into a basic abstract in
the form of a coloured shape. Having done this the mind is then in
a position to control the condition and reverse the negative,
destructive psychosomatic force into a positive creative one and so
bring about healing. Although as self-healing this is a consciously

controlled exercise, our dreaming mind often does this spontaneously and it can be requested to do so by incubation.

As well as representing physical and mental conditions, shapes and colours also convey principles, energies and moods. Red, for example, always symbolizes physical energy, like hard work, energy-drive and sex. Sometimes it reflects anger, as in the case of 'a red rag to a bull'. Violet, on the other hand, symbolizes spiritual things and green, the colour in the middle of the light spectrum represents emotions. The meaning and association of these colours is traditionally inherited from the collective unconscious and they apply not only in dream symbolism but to everything else in life generally. Green, for example, has instinctively been recognized and used as an emotionally stabilizing colour, hence hospital wards and classrooms were once decorated throughout in this colour.

Colour is important in dreams and the role it played in the following dream is interesting although the message it conveyed was not, at first glance, obvious. In this particular dream the dreamer saw the road outside his house as being blood-red, suggesting some sort of physical warning. On noticing that he lived in 'Redpath Road', the real truth dawned. This lay in the name of the road, which for some reason had become symbolized in his dream. Having brought this to light and recognized it as a play on words, the dreamer admitted that the name did in fact emanate a nasty feeling which vaguely worried him. Probably the association of blood on the road and thoughts of accidents upset him but by seeing it in this way, hopefully, he could come to terms with it.

Puns

The best therapy for depression is laughter and the greatest therapists are comedians who dispense much of their treatment through joking puns. Whether these are thought up consciously or whether they come to comedians' minds spontaneously I do not know but one thing is certain: dreaming minds love puns and can conjure them up easily if and when the need arises. A few days before I was due to give a talk on dreams I dreamed for three nights running about a particularly weak-looking horse. Thinking purely symbolically, the weak horse represented lack of energy but by concentrating on this aspect only I completely missed the warning pun sign. On the morning of the talk I awoke with a hoarse voice and although the lack of energy symbol could be made to fit the interpretation, if I had recognized the warning properly I could probably have staved off the hoarseness.

Dreaming minds love to play clever games with words in other ways too, reflecting our waking life which is dominated by conversations rich in anecdotes, innuendos and double meanings. Words in themselves are symbolic anyway and the art of reading depends on recognizing them as such. When we consciously see the word 'cat' we unconsciously see in our mind's eye a cat, just as the word 'car' conjures up a mind-picture of a car. The conversion of words into symbols when awake, whether read or spoken, is, however, reversed in dreams. Here, it is the symbol we are left with, the mirror-image situation, and it is this that has to be converted back into words!

Linguistic Dreams

When we learn a language we inherit the wisdom of generations. for language, like everything else, has evolved over the centuries. Every word is a symbol, a symbol that can either be spoken or written, with both offering a sensory stimuli. To our minds, words act as triggers and relate to one of our five senses, thus becoming a visual, feeling, hearing, smelling or tasting word-picture. And in reverse we use experiences from these stored sensory impressions to describe situations and circumstances.

When we think in terms of a visual word-picture we use dialogue and phrases to match, like 'let's look at it this way', 'focus attention on the problem', and 'see it like this'. Other times we may use a feeling word-picture so we say things like 'I can't handle this', 'take the rough with the smooth' and 'get a grip on ourselves'. If it is auditory thinking then the conversation will include phrases like 'that rings a bell', 'it sounds like hard work' and 'pay up to the tune of £50.00'.

Seeing, hearing and feeling are the three senses we use most to describe life, but the senses of smell and taste are by no means left out verbally. How about the situation from which we hope to emerge 'smelling of roses' or the not so pleasant one where 'we smell a rat'? For taste, when it comes to word-pictures, we often talk about 'the bitterness of some people' and 'the gall of others', not to mention 'good and bad taste in clothes'.

Since we use such picturesque language when awake, with each word passing its linguistic image back and forth across that same bridge frequented by the dreaming mind, just think what the dreaming mind can conjure up. By using exactly the same language we use during the day, is it surprising that we take ourselves literally at night! The following dream shows that we certainly do this! This dream came from a housewife who did not understand the message until it was applied honestly to herself and to circumstances which only she knew. The dream began with a loud knocking on the dreamer's front door and when she opened it she found a big fat cow standing there with a milk jug dangling on the end of its tail. Now the big cow obviously represented someone whom the dreamer was in the habit of calling just that. The truth was that a neighbour frequently knocked loudly on the door to borrow tea, sugar and, of course, milk, and having called her a big fat cow so often, her dreaming mind reflected it back as a stark visual image.

Premonition Dreams

The majority of dreams are by no means profound truths or startling prophecies although all have their message and meaning. Life is full of trivia posing trivial problems so it is to be expected that our dreams trade heavily in these too. Shopping, walking, office filing and the many other routine and boring tasks can all be reassessed and reflected in dreams but for the most part the really insignificant ones are soon forgotten. Dreams reflect the person and his lifestyle so if we lead boring lives then we have boring dreams or remember none of them because there is not much to remember. If, on the other hand, our lives are full of ambition, enthusiasm and creativity, then our dreams will likewise mirror all this and more. Even so, run of the mill dreams still bring minor warnings and can be insignificantly prophetic, showing, if nothing else, that the context of a dream is very different from and has nothing whatsoever to do with the type of dream.

When premonitions are mentioned, one immediately thinks of some world-shattering event having been foreseen in a dream. Several people dreamed of the sinking of the Titanic, the coming of the Second World War and political assassinations but what is not realized is that the majority of premonitions are as trivial as the time they foresaw that the milkman would leave only two pints of milk next Wednesday instead of three. These insignificant yet still prophetic dreams are far more common than most realize. How often the odd word said during the day invokes the memory of the previous night's dream. 'That's broken my dream,' we say instantly, showing we had a premonition, albeit insignificant.

Although incidents like this appear to be of little value there may be more to even them than meets the eye. Take the following example where a lady had a dream featuring an umbrella, and little else. When she awoke she found it was raining so she collected her umbrella from the cupboard and as she did so she remembered her dream. The umbrella, in turn, reminded her of the last time she used it which happened to be a date with a rather handsome man whom she had not seen or thought about since. This triggered off the response to phone him and in three months she had married him!

Although prophetic dreams can help in a dozen or more different ways including preparing us for the imminent death of relatives or even mere acquaintances, many still appear to serve no useful purpose whatsoever. Maybe we have to wait a long while before their significance is recognized, by which time we will probably have forgotten them. It was just such a dream I had in 1963 that decided for me that dreams were meant to play an important part in my life, although its prophetic content could not in any way alter events that later came true. All it did was to prove to me, quite conclusively, that there were definitely such things as prophetic dreams.

The dream was in 1963, following a tour of American hospitals with a group of British radiographers. During this I managed to sandwich in a very brief meeting with an aunt who lived in St Louis but I did not go to her home, she came to see me in Minneapolis. About six weeks after returning home I had a spectacular dream showing this aunt pacing up and down her backyard, as she called it, in a furious distraught state. She told me clearly in this dream that the cause of her anger was a man called Grayson. This so impressed me that I wrote to her at once asking if anything was wrong and if she knew of anyone called Grayson. She soon replied saying she was fine and that she had never heard of anyone called Grayson, so I forgot all about it until, that is, she came to London two years later. On meeting her, she immediately thrust my letter about the dream into my hand. What had happened was that one year after she received it she found herself in a terrible rage, pacing up and down her backyard. Apparently, a new boss had taken over where her husband worked and sacked all the older men, which understandingly made my aunt extremely angry. To let off steam she went out into her backyard where here her memory must have rung some sort of bell because she suddenly remembered my letter which she had kept. Reading it over she was staggered to discover the name Grayson. This was the name of the new boss!

At the time I had this dream the man in question was totally unknown not only to me and my aunt but to her husband as well, so this completely rules out telepathic communication as a possible explanation.

Sugar Ray Robinson
Another dream that sadly came true despite the dreamer's efforts to divert the course of destiny happened in 1947, in the boxing ring. Just before Sugar Ray Robinson's welter-weight title fight with Jimmy Doyle, Robinson dreamed that during the fight one of his punches killed Doyle. His manager and a priest assured him that dreams simply did not come true but they were wrong. What these advisers should have said was that dreams do not *always* come true, but in the eighth round this one did and the warning dream became prophetic.

Dream Telepathy
Telepathy, often called mind reading, is direct communication between two people on a mind or psychic level. When awake this happens coincidentally or apparently so, and spontaneously in

sleep. Many of our dreams may, in fact, be direct telepathic messages from another person, spirit or some unidentifiable source and these, acting as external stimuli, are transformed by our own dreaming mind into meaningful and not so meaningful dream scenes. Just as we communicate on the verbal level when awake, it seems we communicate on a psychic level when asleep and evidence certainly points to the fact that messages do come into our heads from the outside. If we are all linked on the collective unconscious level, as suggested by C. G. Jung, then this would by no means be impossible.

Experiments carried out in dream laboratories show that telepathic communication is far more successful when we are asleep than when we are awake. This being so, it is more than likely that in sleep we pick up thoughts from others, so some dreams may well be someone else's dream! The priests of old were capable of dreaming for others and Daniel had no difficulty in re-dreaming Nebuchadnezzar's half-forgotten dream, by picking up impressions relating to others, so why not us?

Mind Reading Lovers
All the world loves a lover and the reason for this is that when we are madly in love we are happier, more relaxed and, above all, much more tolerant of others. But being in love is more than this. It is a near psychic state. The world becomes a magical Garden of Eden and that is when we are wide awake! In sleep and in dreams the universe is ours. During wars or in times of forced separation the two-way link is so strong that twin dreaming is quite usual, with identical dreams being shared and sometimes, one lover dreams the first part of a dream, with the partner dreaming the sequel.

Psychic or Incubus Attacks
Another aspect of thought transference in dreams is that we pick up stray thoughts that are negative or, even worse, receive those aimed specifically at us, against our will. These cause terrible nightmares known as psychic or incubus attacks and children are especially vulnerable. Usually, terrifying black shapes, shadows and creepie-crawlie things are described as insinuating their way

into their dreams. An incubus, by definition, is an evil spirit that descends on those asleep and attempts to possess or take over and influence the dreamer's thoughts. This definition covers a multitude of sins of course, from impressions received from malevolent ghosts to the reception of strong, dominant thoughts specifically projected to the dreamer from a person who wishes them harm.

These attacks have been recognized for centuries and there have always been ways of protecting against them. The Victorians favoured prayers picked out in needlework cross-stitch which they hung above their beds, whilst others preferred a picture of Jesus on the wall and a crucifix under their pillow. As external symbols of divine power these help tremendously but are only secondary compared with taking responsibility for our own protection. After all, if we take the trouble to protect ourselves at night from intruders on a practical level by bolting doors and windows, why not on a psychic and mental level too?

Psychic Protection

As a guard against these attacks there is a simple and effective mental ritual that keeps out unwanted influences and stimuli, including bad telepathic thoughts from others. This protection depends on the energy field surrounding us, composed of heat, sound and electrical impulses plus a subtler force field usually referred to as the aura. It is a blend of these that protects us but if we are tired, rundown, ill or depressed, this barrier becomes drained and is insufficient to keep all at bay. The aim, therefore, of this exercise is to build up this positive energy field.

This should be carried out just before going to sleep, so having settled down warmly in bed, lie flat on your back, close your eyes and breathe in to the count of two, and out to the count of three or even four, thus imitating the sleep breathing rhythm. To relax physically turn your attention to both feet and clench up the toes for a second or two and then relax them. Next, move both ankles a little and turn up your toes towards your head and then let them go. Think of your knees and thighs as resting. Now turn your attention to your hands and clench your fists and then relax them. Concentrate next on your spine as it relaxes, and your shoulders too. Feel the gravitational forces anchoring you to the bed, holding you there like a magnet. Think now of your face and know that all the lines and furrows have gone and your face is young and smooth.

You will now be relaxed and ready to carry out that simple self-protection ritual. In your mind's eye see that energy field around you. See it as a blue, white or gold light that completely envelops you as a protective cloak and know that inside it you are utterly safe. Nothing can penetrate that barrier. It is as simple as that so please try it if ever the need arises.

Children who have recurring nightmares, where the same frightening entity scares them night after night, are helped if given some coloured crayons and paper and asked to draw the nasty apparition that scares them so. When they have done this, which I might add is usually drawn in grey or black, tell them that these things love the dark so right over them get the child to draw a big, strong, yellow sun, sending its rays of light into all the dark corners. This reduces fear tremendously and by introducing it as a game and placing funny hats on the thing, their confidence grows and with it their positivity and natural protection. On a purely practical level though, if a light is kept on, even a small one, it is found that many such nightmares are prevented, anyway!

Healing Thoughts

Thoughts are projections of energy and, like all forms of energy, can be used for good or bad, depending on their origin and intention. Negative thoughts in the form of external stimuli produce nightmares and psychic attacks but the complete reverse of this is possible, too. When we are asleep we are far more receptive to external stimuli, protection apart, for the simple reason that we are less aware of our five physical senses that flood our minds when awake. We might as well, therefore, make use of the positive forces, which are there as well as the negative.

Healing is given in our dreams in a variety of ways. Some produce practical solutions which when tried work wonders, so as sources of solace we can be sure that dreams are there waiting to be of service to us. Sometimes it seems to be more of a waking experience than a dream, where the spirit of a doctor who died years ago appears at a patient's bedside and dispenses healing potions. On waking there is always much improvement in the patient's condition which they link directly with the help brought to them in the night by the strange spectre. Many hospitals, not surprisingly, have their healing ghosts and the most famous is the Grey Lady at St Thomas's Hospital in London who has been seen by nurses and a former matron as well as by many patients. This lady ghost ministers through their dreams to sleeping patients who, on waking, find themselves well on the road to recovery.

The Scottish GP

Not all these dream doctors and nurses, however, are the spirits of the dead departed. In some inexplicable way the thoughts of some very much alive people are able to contact and convey healing to others even though they do not even know the person they are helping. When Tudor Pole, a well-known archaeologist, writer and psychic, was in Egypt before the war he was struck down with a virulent fever. At the time he was on a houseboat on the River Nile and as he dozed and dreamed he heard a loud knocking on his cabin door. A British doctor entered, dressed in a black coat and striped trousers, the accepted dress for doctors in those days, and prescribed something for the tropical malady. Tudor Pole was fascinated by the doctor's hat which he had placed on a table. He could see right through it. The doctor explained he was in practice in Britain and that he often left his body in sleep to travel to whomsoever he was sent. A feverish fancy, some might say, but such beliefs were far from Tudor Pole's mind. When he returned to England he appealed on BBC radio for the doctor to come forward. He did; he was a general practitioner in Scotland who confirmed that he did indeed leave his body during sleep to visit patients in need of help.

So much can happen in our dreams, with and without persuasion, but since it is possible to tune into positive forces there is no reason why we should not request help and healing from them, exactly as they did in the long distant past. Praying for assistance to come in a dream is a form of incubation and many dreamers are rewarded with visits not only from incarnate doctors and the ghosts of merciful nurses but with visions of Jesus, the Great Healing Spirit, Himself.

Flying Dreams

Every night when we sleep there are those among us who, like the Scottish G.P., apparently leave their bodies and travel to far-off places. Forty-five out of every hundred people, when asked, said they had experienced this at least once in their lives and some actually travelled like this regularly each night. Dreams of weightlessness, flying over roof-tops as we flap our arms like wings, floating horozintally a few feet above the ground and leaping like astronauts on the moon are perhaps more nocturnal happenings than dreams and are known as out of the body experiences or astral projections. This suggests that part of us, our astral, or etheric body, or ghost in the machine as some call it, actually leaves the physical body. The practical theorists believe this all to be due to an inherited ancestral memory from the days when, according to Darwin's theory, our predecessors were aquatic or airborne creatures. Psychologists prefer to call it depersonalization, which is only another name for it but explains nothing.

These explanations fade in the light of other evidence showing that during these flights irrefutable evidence, as in the case of the Scottish doctor, has been brought back to prove that the dreamer, in some shape or form, did visit those far-off places. In 1948 a lady in England, whose daughter had emigrated to Australia, flew in her dream to her daughter's bedside in Brisbane where she found her to be seriously ill. On waking the dreamer phoned her daughter who confirmed she was ill but even more staggering was the fact that she had woken in the night and seen her mother standing by her bedside. Telepathic communication could explain some but not all of these experiences, so who can say, for sure, what the answer is?

Dream Lovers

We all have the latent image of the man or woman of our dreams but unfortunately they do not always materialize as the great lover we have kept hidden and perhaps searched for for so long. Sometimes we dream prophetically of this partner, recognizing definite features about them when we meet in the flesh. Romance apart, this certainly points to a pre-set destiny for dream lovers, if not for others!

Many dreams concerning making love to a neighbour or a person whom we hardly know are a kind of mind game where candidates for the perfect partner are tried out in confidence and secrecy. In six months one lady dreamer worked through all the men on the side of her street, the odd numbered side! One wonders how often such dreams are reciprocated through telepathic communication but this is something we shall never know. Not many of us would admit to ourselves let alone to others that we found a particular person attractive so when the unshackled mind thinks it is necessary, it conjures up a nice little passionate dream scene to show the conscious self what the rest of us really feels. Hardly a wish-fulfilment dream, more a projection of the truth but if the dream is repeated then it could be sublimation for the real thing. It could, of course, be prophetic!

Dancing in dreams, is a prelude to love-making. Ladies dream far more of dancing with the romantic figure of a man and having a kiss and a cuddle but men dream more of having straight, fulfilling sex on the floor without any frills and not much romance. This shows the different approaches of the sexes, the active more practical let's-have-it-now of the male and the wait-for-a-bit romantic female.

Guilt Dreams

No one ever dreams of having sex with one's regular bed partner if sex is there for the asking or taking because there is no need. On the other hand, when it is not there we have to concede that Freud was right with his wish-fulfilment and sublimation interpretations. Having sex in public places like the middle of the supermarket is by no means rare, in dreams of course, and it shows quite clearly that the dreamer is suffering from some form of guilt complex, but not necessarily sexual. A recent dream I interpreted led me to believe that the sex the dreamer had in a supermarket amid the canned was more an act of diversion than perversion. What with helping herself and being in the soup, shoplifting was symbolically implied far more than anything else.

Just as Freud thought ordinary objects were disguised sex symbols I have found that sex, as a symbol in its own right, stands for ordinary or rather extraordinary activities far removed from love-making. Apart from shoplifting, sex in dreams represented male dominance in business, arising no doubt from the popular saying 'Get stuffed'. I have also found it represents female jealousy and one-upmanship generally.

If we decide a sex dream is mainly literal then the message probably applies to our sex lives and our outlook on this subject. Symbolically, snakes are a favourite sex symbol but, in fact, they represent energy drives generally and since sex is only one of those drives, the context in which the snake appears gives the clue to the level of energy it represents. They can, therefore, indicate ambitions, temptations, hidden powers, secret activities, forces of nature, and healing ability, or down-to-earth deviousness like the proverbial snake in the grass.

Recurring Dreams

The dream that recurs time and time again does so simply because its message has not been received and understood. Once it is, it stops immediately for its work is done. Some dreamers have experienced the same dream, on and off, since childhood, with the same old record being played time and time again. Others, however, experience them over shorter periods, with repeats covering only a few weeks or months. One lady had a recurring nightmare from earliest childhood and in these she was always alone in a deep pit. From behind a rock a lion would suddenly appear and spring at her, at which point she would wake up screaming! It was not until she was quite old, and still having virtually the same nightmare at two to three monthly intervals, that I explained the possibility that these could be action-replays from a previous life, where she had, in fact, been thrown to the lions. At first she rejected this as outright nonsense because she did not believe in reincarnation. As time went by, however, she warmed to the idea and finally accepted that it might just be possible. From then on the nightmares ceased.

In no way does this prove reincarnation but what it does prove is that the explanation was sufficient to put an end to a deep-seated fear. To know the devil is to overcome it and there is more than one devil! Hypnosis, once believed to be infallible and reveal only truthful past events, has been proved to substitute explanations for phobias and fears, so if reasonable they can replace the original misnomer and all will be well. Wrong association of ideas with memories filed in the wrong place is the usual explanation and in fact the lady with the bad lion dream may have been re-enacting a tale told to her at far too young an age! Either way, the ghost of the fearful lion was laid.

Scheming Dreams

It is often asked why dreams are so scheming, devious and complicated and the answer is that they are not. There is nothing in them that we have not put there ourselves, even though some may have been triggered off by external stimuli. Dreams reveal, they do not conceal. The complexities of life today are such that we do not have enough time to solve our problems before going to sleep so consequently much of our dream-time is taken up with action-replays and symbolically reflected dreams showing mixed-up situations. Although dreams are well able to help us out in this way, if we leave too much for them to sort out it does not give our dreaming mind time to pass on those original messages that have the power to inspire and motivate the genius within. The mere fact of realizing that this is possible is often all that is needed to alter a life-long pattern of closed circuit dreaming, and when this happens we are then ready to try out Kekule's famous message of learning to dream!

5

INTERPRETATIONS AND SOLUTIONS FROM DREAMS

Before we can interpret dreams we must first have material on which to work, so for this we need to keep a dream diary. It was Edgar Casey's son Hugh Lyn who said that the best book we shall ever read on dreams is the one we write ourselves. He was, of course, referring to our personal dream diary. Many people conscientiously keep a most orderly account of their boring day-time happenings yet never consider recording their nightlife which, if they did but know it, is far more instructive, interesting and exciting!

The Dream Diary
There are no hard and fast rules relating to dreams, even when it comes to keeping a record of them, but it helps to have a few practical guidelines.

Rule 1: The Diary
The first rule in keeping a dream diary is very practical indeed but at the same time ritualistic. It is this. Go out and buy an attractive notebook and pen expressly for this purpose. This is the first commitment too and as an act of faith it alerts the dreaming mind to the fact that we really mean business. Once having bought these, place them by the bedside where they must at all costs stay because if they wander we cannot possibly afford to hunt for them

in the middle of the night when they are most needed. We might find them but at the expense of losing a valuable dream.

Rule 2: The Number, the Date and the Time

The second rule concerns the numbering, dating and if possible noting the time of each dream. It is important that the day and the date are clearly written at the top of a fresh page each night in readiness with the merit in this becoming more and more apparent as we continue to do so, for it is only in retrospect that some warnings can be seen and prophecies recognized. Dating also reveals sequences and series of dreams, and recurring dreams plus many other surprising features, not least being the revelation that the dreaming mind is a fantastic calendar and clock. Forgotten birthdays, anniversaries and events that happened long ago on that date are remembered and even events that are to happen in the future may be indicated, too. Numbering dreams in the order of appearance is also important. Some nights there will be more than one to record so continue with the numerical sequence. If the time of the dream is known or rather the waking time coinciding with it, this should be recorded too.

Rule 3: Speed

The third rule is that we must write down all we can remember about a dream or dreams immediately on waking and this means before we have thought of or done anything else whatsoever. Dreams fade very quickly and many can be captured only by putting them down on paper at once. This fading of dreams is another reason why so many people vow they never dream but they would be amazed to discover they did, if they followed the simple but vital rule of putting pen to paper instantly they opened their eyes! If, however, a dream does initially evade us it nevertheless leaves an impression behind in the form of a particular mood, feeling or atmosphere, so note this.

Rule 4: Filling-in

The fourth rule is to fill in all the gaps. It takes considerable will-power to snatch a pen at 2 a.m. in the morning but believe it or not this soon becomes an exciting habit. It also serves to keep our dreaming mind informed that we still mean serious business. Hopefully, most dream recording can be done first thing in the morning but whatever the time, never mind the scribble. This can be sorted out later in the harsh light of day, the vital thing is to record as much as we can remember, as fast as possible.

When we have done all this we are then in possession of a good rough sketch but this needs going over, there and then, for missed details. A time delay at this stage robs us of valuable evidence so on this second time around look for any colours that stand out, remembering that colours fade first and faster than other parts of the dream, hence the belief that some dreams are in black and white. Look, too, for conversation pieces, words, songs or poems plus everything that comes to mind. Having added this we now write down anything that reminds us of an event from the previous day, such as a TV programme, a conversation, an incident, a worry, or a problem we have on our mind. These associations are priceless when it comes to the interpretation.

Finally, make a list of all signs and symbols. These will be in the form of people, animals, monsters, objects, shapes and universal archetypes including religious and mysterious symbols.

At an appropriate moment during the next day the night's dream has to be tidied up, probably re-written and put in some order in readiness for interpretation. Scrap paper, incidentally, can be used for that first rough draft and then the final version can be written neatly into the dream diary later. This means that scrap paper has to be already placed in the diary but it is well worth the extra effort especially if we have to write in the dark which is often the case if we do not want to, or dare not, disturb someone else!

The important features entered in a dream diary will, therefore, include the following, in this order: The number, date and time of the dream. *The Dream itself*. The atmosphere, feeling or mood and any colours it left behind. Special conversation pieces, words, songs or poems. A list of signs and symbols. Previous associations. The finished product of a night's dreaming could look something like the page from my dream diary, for the night of 17 March 1983, showing two very different dreams. Incidentally, if we think daytime diaries are revealing they are nothing compared with their night-time counterpart waiting to emerge!

<u>Date</u>: Thursday 17 March 1983

<u>Dream Number</u>: 40

<u>Time</u>: Don't know but before 6 a.m.

<u>THE DREAM</u>: I was trying to do up a necklace but had great difficulty in doing so. A voice said quite distinctly 'Try, try, try again.'

<u>Atmosphere</u>: Ordinary.

<u>Mood</u>: Alert.

<u>Signs and Symbols</u>: Necklace.

<u>Words</u>: Try, try, try again.

<u>Previous Associations</u>: Seen bank statement yesterday and wondered how to make ends meet.

<u>Dream Number</u>: 41

<u>Time</u>: Between 6 a.m. and 8 a.m.

<u>THE DREAM</u>: I was walking with someone on a hill and saw a large brown friendly snake rolling happily down the hillside. We walked down and when we reached more level ground I noticed some really bright yellow flowering shrubs and some almost unnaturally mauve flowers. In the dream I recognized them as Laburnum and an early flowering shrub called Daphne. I was also aware that it was a dream so I decided there and then to answer some of the questions asked by Dr Keith Herne in his questionnaire on lucid dreaming. One of these I knew was 'Are the colours in your dream (a) brighter than in real life (b) the same as in real life (c) less bright than in real life? I decided they were exactly the same. I then wanted to show the person I was with the snake but could not find it.

<u>Atmosphere</u>: Nice, bright and sunny.

Mood: Happy and inquisitive.

Signs and Symbols: A person, a friend. A hillside and level ground, unrecognized. A large brown friendly snake. Brightly coloured flowers.

Words: None spoken but plenty of thoughts.

Names: Daphne and Dr Keith Herne.

Previous Associations: Dr Herne's project.

The Incubation of Dreams

By keeping a dream diary it soon becomes clear that the majority of our dreams are concerned with practical matters and psychological relationships and only rarely do they spontaneously come to our aid to solve a specific problem. The ancient races recognized dreams as great sources of enlightenment and so took steps to link individual minds with God and lesser divinities whom they looked upon as His messengers. By attuning themselves to one of these deities they requested a dream that would help them with their problems. This form of dream incubation was appropriate to that bygone age but today there are no shrines dedicated to Morpheus nor are there oracular priests who will assist us to dream to order. This, however, does not mean that the age of dream miracles is past. Far from it, but we live in a different age now, one where we must make our own contacts and incubate our own dreams.

The powers that be have certainly not deserted us although we may have deserted them. The gods and goddesses, angels and God's messengers are still very much with us, if we look, for they are those forces Jung called the universal archetypes. Nor are we without oracles; our own dreaming mind is exactly this. By tuning in to ourselves, we can therefore request and receive answers and help just as surely as our ancestors once did.

Dreaming is an art and like most arts it needs practice. True, we all dream and often receive help from dreams at the right time but this is more by luck than judgment compared with what can be achieved if we put ourselves out. Since most of us are content to leave it all to our dreaming mind, what more should we expect than the usual run of the the mill dreams concerned with everyday matters and only the occasional fantastic experiences? If, however, we consciously co-operate with our dreaming mind it is so pleased to be recognized, not to mention surprised, that it becomes our obedient servant overnight!

Self-help and Self-reliance

Self-reliance is a quality of life that has been trodden underfoot and trampled on for too long yet common sense must tell us that there is no living being who can possibly help us, practical things apart, other than ourselves. Just as no one else can digest our food for us, nor can they solve our problems. Our life is always our own responsibility. With dreams we are working entirely with ourselves thus making it an excellent exercise in self-reliance, and since dreams are messages from ourselves to ourselves, this makes a lot of sense.

It has often been said that God helps those who help themselves and this was never truer than when applied to the incubation of dreams. The untapped potential of our mental resources is more than enough to keep us safe and secure, not to mention healthy and wise, but who can wonder that we receive so little help from this source when we barely recognize its existence let alone its power. Through our dreams all is possible and if we need proof of this we have only to look back at history and at the more recent examples of help brought about by the power of dreams. If others can do it, some by design and some by apparent chance, then so can we.

The incubation of dreams simply means asking our dreaming mind for help but even in this day and age where we are the oracle and the dreamer we still need a mental ritual to co-ordinate ourselves with archetypal forces. Each of us, however, must go about this in the way that suits us best. If we feel we would rather rely entirely on God then the request for a special dream should be made in the form of an invocative prayer. All religions tell us that God speaks to us through our dreams so there is no reason why we should not ask for His help in this way. On the other hand, by appealing to our innermost selves, that part of us some call the soul or spirit, we can receive equally good results. Maybe the answers and stimuli come from the same divine source, who knows, we are all part of the Creation, after all.

Head and Heart Again

The time to incubate dreams is when we are in bed, warm, relaxed and ready to go to sleep. The difficulty though is often relaxing. When a problem churns round and round in the head relaxation is the one thing we cannot achieve. Advice like 'Don't worry' is worse than useless so it has to be tackled from an entirely different standpoint. It helps, I find, if we say, 'I can't solve it intelligently with my head when awake so I might as well let the intuition of my heart have a go when asleep, so over to you, dreaming mind.' This works well, for it off-loads or shifts responsibility from one part of us to another which is better equipped to take the burden. Having carried out this silent verbal ritual concentrate now on relaxing physically, as follows.

The Relaxing Exercise

Lie flat on your back and think of both feet. Clench your toes and then let them relax. Then waggle both ankles and let them go. Turn up your toes towards your head and then relax them. Think now of both hands and clench your fists, and let them go. Concentrate now on your spine and think of it being straight, and without pressure from above. The gravitational pull is now at right angles compared with when standing up so there is no weight upon it. It is relaxed. Think of the gravitational force that anchors you to the bed as energy, which is what it is, and feel it charge you up and link you with the natural forces of the planet.

The Mental Ritual

If we are still awake after this then now is the time to begin the incubation of a dream. To do this we must contact that part of us which is responsible for sending us dreams and speak to it silently but positively, like this: 'Please, dreaming mind, send me a dream that will help me.' Into this request we incorporate pleas like 'please give me a sign; please direct energy to that part of me that needs healing; tell me how I can best help those who ask for my help, or what shall I do?' Each plea will be different, of course, but the sharper and more concise we can make it the more cut and dried will be the response. Rambling requests receive rambling replies. Having made our request in the most concise way possible we now tell ourselves that we are ready and waiting to receive a message and that we are going to write down all we can remember about the dream immediately on waking. Positive affirmation, on the other hand, works well and a request from this standpoint would be along these lines: 'Dreaming mind, I expect you to deliver to me a clear dream giving me the answer to the question I am going to ask you. I am ready for this and I will write down every detail you send to me.'

How we incubate our dreams is up to us entirely with much depending on our way of life and our religious beliefs, but probably a different approach for different situations is best. Whichever way we choose, this is what Professor Kekule meant when he told his students to first learn to dream. How right he was, but practice makes perfect so do not be too disappointed if at first you do not succeed. You will, if you keep up the impetus. Finally, when a special dream has been received we must always remember to thank God, the powers that be and ourselves, for sending it to us.

The Interpretation of Dreams

The best person to interpret dreams is none other than the dreamer himself. After all, he alone constructed them using props from his own private store of memories, experiences and associations. This, however, is not to say that someone else cannot interpret them for us at face value because they can. But this is only half the story. Having been given a message, it is then up to the dreamer to apply this to his own personal set of circumstances which he alone knows. Then, and only then, will the interpretation be complete and of any real value.

When Joseph interpreted Pharaoh's dream he did not know how the message of seven years of plenty followed by seven years of famine could or would be put into practice. It took Pharaoh with his experience and association of ideas to understand the full implication of that message and set in motion that which the dream intended.

The more dreams we investigate, our own and others, the more we learn to understand them but there is one trap into which we must not fall and that is when interpreting dreams for others, we do not impose upon them our own association of ideas. We have built these up from unique, personal experiences and they only apply to our own dreams, not other people's dreams. As dream analysts we are able to recognize the literal and symbolic content, see puns and double meanings, translate signs and symbols, all of which give us an overall message, but this is still meaningless to everyone else except the dreamer. It is up to them, ourselves when it is our own dreams we are interpreting, to link this face-value meaning with secret inner knowledge, in order to bring about that alchemical fusion between the dream and reality.

To interpret dreams two qualifications are necessary. One is that we must have a true desire to do so and the other is that we have enough enthusiasm to sustain that desire. To remember and analyse the odd dream here and there is one thing but to really get to grips with them is quite another matter. To do this we have to make a personal commitment but this is most rewarding for we soon learn so much more about ourselves, our pecking order in society and even our place in the universe. If 'Know Thyself' means anything at all then there is no better way of seeking this than through our own dreams.

Having started a personal dream diary we will soon be in possession of at least one well-recorded dream, remembering that whichever type of dream it is, from the mundane to the esoteric, the same basic principles of interpretation will apply. In some dreams it will be the atmosphere that is all important whilst in others it will be the dialogue that stands out. Each dream, however, will be uniquely different and this, along with its other dominant qualities is what we need to discover or uncover, as the case may be.

The Feel of a Dream

Feelings speak louder than words; they are also difficult to put into words so the first step towards interpreting a dream is to discover its feeling, mood or atmosphere. This can be seen as the backcloth on the stage of dreams before which all else is arranged. Props are set up, actors and actresses appear and the action takes place. Sometimes the feeling is all that is left and although getting out of bed the wrong side in the morning is often blamed for a dark mood shadowing us all day this is really due to a hangover from a forgotten dream. This left-over mood is not always negative; it can be positive, extremely cheerful and full of confidence in which case we feel great and happy that the cloud from yesterday has lifted. This is because we have slept on it, as the saying goes and although the details of the night's dreaming were not consciously remembered the sum total of their workings-out, in the shape of a feeling, were. In this we can see the power our dreams have in colouring the next day in our life, if not our entire future.

The feel of a dream is a message in itself. The setting under the midday sun can only evoke a scene of hope and sunnier days for the future but, on the other hand, what an abject picture of misery the gloomy, half-light paints of heavy depression. The atmosphere is accurately reflected in colours and shades of light and dark. Generally, bright light colours denote positive ambitions and enthusiasm for a specific project whereas sombre darker tones tend to indicate weightier, worrying problems full of lost hopes and negativity. Look closely, therefore, at feelings, moods and atmospheres, which includes weather conditions, before all else because if this is missed at the beginning it can mean that the whole interpretation is based on a false premise or, worse, none at all.

The Artist Within

The next task is to decide how much of a dream is literal, and how much is symbolic. If we visit an art gallery we see three types of paintings – literal, symbolic and those which are a mixture of both. The comparison between these and dreams is striking, so it helps to think about a dream as a painting before considering characters, action and dialogue.

The literal painting depicts a true-to-life scene as clearly as any photograph and like its literal dream counterpart, nothing is left to the imagination. Shops are shops, houses are houses, people are themselves and trees are trees right down to the last twig. The artist who painted this is clever but uninspired, using only his head and intellect to impart his message which lies clearly in the importance of the details we miss and take for granted as we rush blindly by. Its title is unimaginative, too, like 'The High Street' and as such belongs to that outer world in which we roam each day.

At first glance the symbolic or abstract painting, like its comparative dream, looks a right mess, meaningless to all who pass by except, that is, to the artist. Splashes of violent colours racing across the canvas produce a riot of shapes and shadows and all attempts to see it as a conventional picture fail hopelessly, at least until the creator of this masterpiece explains that the angry red splashes are yesterday's rage, the dark shadows are today's threats and the gold and white lines are rays of hope for the future. We now see and feel a symbolic cry, not from the head but from the heart. The title, like the painting, is subtle: 'The Turmoil'. One wonders how the High Street artist would paint an inner scene like a turmoil!

The third painting, and many dreams are like this, is a literal and symbolic mixture. Its title, 'The Eyes and Ears of The World', suitably describes a recognizable though monstrous symbolic female with eyes at the back of her head and an ear to the ground. This artist has blended fact with fiction cleverly, probably inaccurately and certainly cruelly to represent his own biased, personal in every sense of that word, view of his mother-in-law. We can see, once we know what to look for, how his mind grabbed at the outer world for obvious signs and then dived down into secret inner recesses in search of a few symbols in order to concoct this rather nasty, albeit accurate, literal and symbolic, caricature.

The dreaming mind is definitely the artist within. The difference, though, between the dream artist and the other artist is that the inner artist has unlimited talent. Using colours in ways the Renoirs, Turners and Michelangelos of this world only dreamed about, the dream artist produces brown studies and blue moods as easily as he or she floods the canvas of the mind with colours from an ethereal rainbow. From the archetypal mystical heights to the abyssmal depths, its power to create is unbelievable.

Signs and Symbols
Signs and symbols are tackled next. These are recognized as

people, animals, objects and designs ranging from an ordinary kitchen mug to an esoteric version of the Holy Grail. There is, however, no definite dividing line between a sign and a symbol because they merge and stand in for each other constantly; generally signs are literal images recognizable as people, animals and real objects but even so this does not mean they necessarily have to be taken at literal face value! More often than not they represent someone or something else, so unless we recognize, say, a horse as the literal sign of a horse in an action-replay dream, it is masquerading as energy in the form of drive and horsepower. Just as a latchkey, unless relating to one lost recently, indicates a clue to a situation or the opening of a door on new opportunities. A ladder, a steamroller, a hammer and a thousand and one other objects are all frequently used by our dreaming mind in much the same way so we must be prepared to recognize them metaphorically and not necessarily literally.

Symbols represent principles and ideas and they always stand for something more than their face value. Sometimes they appear as abstract shapes, mystical designs and religious insignia but mainly they are recognizable signs used as stand-ins. For example, when a horse is used to represent energy or a key a clue they change from signs into symbols. There is little mystery in dream symbology in this respect since most of it comes not from the collective unconscious but from the outer worldly environment flooded with metaphorical words and phrases like 'high horsepower', the 'lion's share', and 'barged into', not to mention the more personal descriptions like 'fiery temper', 'icy manner', 'snake in the grass' and 'silly ass'. Some of these signs-turned-symbols like snakes, for example, were used in this way long before man could read and write so are now traditional symbols bordering on the archetypal. This is where a dictionary helps but most words describing literal images with double meanings need only a little imagination plus personal associations to reveal their hidden message. Take the dream where the dominant sign is a bulldozer. Who could fail to miss the metaphorical implication that someone is about to be forced into uncompromising submission?

Only when a dream is literal can people, animals and objects be interpreted as themselves. Whilst it is not too difficult to see objects and even animals symbolically, it is not easy to see a person as being anything other than themselves, especially if they are close to us. Or is it? After all we are all something as well as someone, to someone else. We are a son or a daughter for a start. Once we take the impersonal viewpoint, which is what the dreaming mind does, we can soon see the game it is playing. People cease to be themselves. They are still recognizable people but as mother, father, daughter, son, grandparent, or friend, they represent not personal individuals, but the impersonal image of the character. Add to this first names, all of which have their own meanings and pet names like chick, ducks and kitten and the faceless circle of impressions widens even more!

Extending this game one step further, we can see why the dreaming mind has little difficulty in finding candidates for projecting the message of idiot, fool, moron or louse!

Parent Figures and Family

Parents and grandparents often put in an appearance in our dreams and as strong as the temptation is to interpret them as themselves, nine times out of ten they are representing principles of an image. Our mothers in a symbolic context represent not themselves but feminine principles of comfort, compassion and sometimes the overbearing powers of the Great Mother earth, whilst our fathers masquerade as the masculine dominance of authority and even the Father image of God Himself. Similarly, a brother or sister represents brotherly or sisterly platonic love.

One step removed from family images is the faceless status symbol. The dustman, the doctor, the typist, the plumber, the nurse and the lawyer, all literally recognized, have their symbolic counterpart so when a policeman turns up in a dream we can bet law and order in our lives are involved.

To sum up then, literal dreams reflecting the outer world use signs like people who play themselves and objects which can be taken at face value. Symbolic dreams reflecting inner thoughts, use literal stand-ins with symbol meanings as well as using purely abstract symbols which include mythological creatures, mazes and universal archetypes. Whatever the sign or symbol it always plays a unique role in each dream but, at the same time, some are used repeatedly to convey, in essence, the same basic meaning. Apart from members of the family being used in this way, so too are houses, water, explosions, animals, trees and cars, trains, boats, aeroplanes, buses and bikes.

Conversation, Words and Dialogue

Often it is not what we say but the way we say it that makes the most impact, so if there is any dialogue in a dream note the intonation first. 'This is a fine state of affairs' may in fact be describing the complete opposite from what has been said and the dreaming mind knows all about this sort of double talk. Words are signs and symbols in themselves so if we cannot take them at face value, we have to interpret them metaphorically. Sometimes though, the message is to be taken literally but the situation is symbolic and one instance of this was the dream I had about trying to do up a necklace. The message of 'Try, try, try again' was to be taken literally whereas the fastening of the necklace was symbolic, representing the situation.

Recently, a lady dreamed she was in a wood and met an elf who said to her, 'The man who chops wood will save you.' A symbolic message if ever there was one! Without knowing her circumstances, I took this to mean that she was in a very indecisive state, in the wood in fact, and the only person who could get her out of it was a positive, practical and probably sexy man. This dreamer replied to say that her problem had been to make a choice between two men in her life and the woodchopper image fitted the description of one but not the other! May they be very happy on the strength of her dream and its meaning!

Puns and Riddles

The dreaming mind produces puns and riddles every bit as good as those found in Christmas crackers, assuring us that we have incredible literary abilities when asleep, if not when awake! Pet names have great punning potential as the man who constantly dreamed of a poor bedraggled chick soon found out. He had never heard of dream puns but if he had he would have recognized his poor little henpecked wife, whom he insisted on calling Chick, sooner.

Body puns, using body language like 'handing over', 'head in that direction', 'get if off your chest', 'let's get to the bottom of things', and 'I can't stand it', are just a few examples of this type. Then there are parable puns like 'putting your foot in it', 'get your oar in there', 'face the music', 'tell it to the Marines', and 'pie in the sky', all of which are easily missed unless we keep our ear to the ground!

Finally, there are some common or garden verbal puns where the names are the same but the spelling is sometimes different. Horse and hoarse, spell and spell, guilt and gilt, shoo and shoe, red and read, sole and soul and heel and heal, are a few examples. One way of exposing these and other puns generally is to read the dream out loud, but on the quiet, of course!

Previous Associations

If a previous association is noted in the dream diary then this is the next aspect to be taken into account. Late-night television is notorious for making its way into dreams but this is not the cause nor the stimulus that triggered it off. Whilst viewing the screen the dreaming mind, like a good journalist, is always on the look-out for original material to incorporate into a dream setting. If, for example, there is a lively skirmish between cowboys and Indians this would serve as a wonderful battleground for a fight between the dreamer and the taxman, who could usefully play the axeman!

Social gatherings are rich sources too, as the man who spent the previous evening in a busy pub, exclusively in male company, found out. His subsequent dream was an action-replay of the pub scene but with one big difference. His friends were not all male, but all female!

The Dream Play

A dream is usually a series of events similar to a play. There are those with many acts and scenes and those centred around one central happening but the main difference is that in dream plays, the dreamer decides on the title, theme and action, writes all the script, puts in the puns, innuendoes and double talk, designs the scenery, arranges the props, casts the actors and actresses and then promptly goes and sits in the front row of the audience to watch.

And when one of the characters in this play is the dreamer, he or she then gets up onto the stage and takes the lead.

Having created these characters, it also follows that the dreamer plays them as well, putting words into their mouths that he would like to hear. If, however, the dreaming mind is impartial, which it can be, then these characters will be portrayed in a much more realistic and not so emotional way. Hopefully, this will lead to better relationships all round.

If, when we read a dream through to look for puns, we look at it as if it were a play, the action and any dialogue will reveal the role each person is playing and with it the overall dream theme also emerges. Themes help to give a title to a dream as well as putting what they are saying into a nutshell. All dreams have individual themes and however long or short the dream, its theme should be expressed as simply and concisely as possible. Even a rambling saga beginning on a cliff top, long-windedly describing the descent of the dreamer to the beach where he watches a tidal wave approach and race towards the shore, inundating and drowning many people, followed by the eventual escape of the dreamer up the cliff to safety, can be summed up in the explicit sentence: 'A threatening situation will or can be overcome.'

The Message and the Solution

Hopefully, all the effort put into unravelling a dream, which includes discovering its backcloths, props, people, signs and symbols, plus recognizing puns and double talk, will unite and transform into a coherent message. Like dreams themselves though, some messages will be short and simple whilst others will be long and less concise.

When a message reveals a difficult situation, as it so often does, a solution or way out is usually to be found in the dream too, and this can be even more important than the message although it is, of course, really part of it. That dream of the on-rushing tidal wave warns of approaching trouble but the message also incorporates the solution which is that the dreamer can rise above it. As a measure of prophecy, comfort can be drawn from this but effort, symbolized by the no doubt difficult climb up a cliff face, must be made to fulfil the message.

Just as a warning dream will remain a warning dream and not end up prophetic if the message is acted upon, so the reverse is true of dreams revealing a problem with a potential solution. The key, in both instances, is to act upon the message, thus preventing or facilitating that which is possible.

Prophecy, Subliminal Perception and Premonitions

In understanding solutions lie the questions of prophecy, subliminal perception and premonitions. Prophecy, it seems, is more an unconscious deduction from subliminal perception where the unconscious mind has registered much more than the conscious mind. The action-replay dream showing how the dreamer misjudged her office colleagues was an example of this, discovering as she did that they were not talking about but her birthday card.

Premonitions, on the other hand, seem to result from extra-sensory perception with no apparent conscious or unconscious link with the past, present, or future and predict events which no living person could possibly have deduced logically beforehand. Even inspired guesses can be ruled out as well as subliminal perception because the true premonition gives names and places and sometimes dates of future events. It is acausal; there is no chain of action and reaction. As meaningless and apparently useless as it was, apart from showing me that there really were such things as premonitions, the dream I had concerning my aunt in St Louis and the man unknown to her and myself at the time, was an example of this type of dream.

A Practical Guide to the Interpretation

Hard and fast rules cannot be applied to the art of interpreting dreams any more than they can to the keeping of a dream diary but if they are investigated against a set plan it makes it much easier to discover what their messages are.

Having noted all the information given in our dream diary we are now ready to begin on the interpretation, and the practical aspect to be noted first is the date of the dream. This may or may not match up with an anniversary. Next, we try to re-create the mood the dream left behind and remember the atmosphere in which it all took place. This will reveal degrees of warning or the reverse, boosts of encouragement and hope for the future. By looking at the dream as if it were a painting it will then be fairly obvious if it is predominantly literal or symbolic but either way, it must first be assumed to have a literal message.

Only when this refuses to fit into the picture should a symbolic or mystical meaning be even considered. Those people who see all their dreams as great mystical truths often spend their lives, literally, in their dreams and never put whatever those great truths are into practice. This is not to deny that their interpretations are wrong but by not associating and anchoring them to their practical everyday life they remain as so much pie-in-the-sky and, as such, are wasted. We must make use of our dreams down here, not marvel at them, up there!

Look, then, for the practical message and its practical application remembering that a dream may well have a double message, one to be taken literally, and one to be listened to symbolically as well. Linking the story or series of events together and seen as a play, much will be revealed. Dialogue, puns and double talk will come to life and with the help of a dream dictionary the more traditional meanings of signs and symbols will be found. Previous associations having been accounted for and the underlying theme discovered, the message should now be recognized. And once having done this all that remains is to apply this to our own personal situation or circumstances, which we alone know.

Dream Themes and the Royal Road

'The interpretations of dreams is the royal road to a knowledge of the subconscious activities of the mind,' said Freud. What he did not know was that the British tend to take this literally and make frequent trips down that road to hob-nob with royalty. Using royalty as a dream theme is far more common than most would care to admit. The Queen, called Lilibet more often than not, accompanied by the Queen Mother, pops in for tea and a chat in Blackpool whilst Princess Anne allows her horse to nibble away at neat lawns in Clapham, Biggleswade, Bognor and Hull.

Illusions of grandeur and thinking one is better than the neighbours apart, the royalty theme symbolizes those archetypal forces we were force-fed on as children. Cinderella, Sleeping Beauty, frogs into princes and kings and queens from endless fairy stories who always end up living happily ever afterwards, are deeply imbedded into our collective unconscious and whether we are royalists or not, the Queen symbolizes the ultimate heroine. She is Venus, the High Priestess, the Queen of Heaven and Mother Earth. She is the personification of the feminine aspect of life itself. The other side of that coin, however, is not so romantic but it is certainly more practical. It is a fact that members of the royal family really do come into our homes and right into our living rooms, on television, so who can blame all those dreaming minds for seizing upon this event as an interesting and symbolic theme.

Just as some signs and symbols are used more frequently than others in dreams, so too are certain themes, royalty being just one of them. We all have these basic-theme dreams from time to time and although in content they are much the same, the messages they convey to the individual dreamer are always different.

The Mansion of the Soul

The most common of these themes is that of a house or building which we nocturnally inhabit. When we are not dreaming literally this symbolizes the Mansion of the Soul. Each dream house is as different as the dreamer who creates it and this represents him or her as a person. The house is the physical counterpart and the occupier is the dreamer's soul or spirit who flits hauntingly through strange yet half-familiar rooms, ascends and descends staircases, glides along corridors and passages, through doors and under archways. Up in the attic are stored high hopes, some forgotten like dusty relics, whereas down in the cellar are creepy-crawlie things that hide in dark corners. The bedroom is for privacy and sex whereas in the kitchen we have to face the practical facts of life. The permutations are endless but the underlying theme is always the same, concerning itself with personal relationships within and around that dream mansion.

The condition of the house, inside and out, reveals physical and mental states of the dreamer. If the action takes place in the attic then ideals, hopes, intuition and intellectual matters are under review but if the scene is set in the cellar then light will have to be shone on the objects hidden away down there. Throughout the house there will be doors of opportunity; some may be locked in which case it is the key we need. Stairs might be difficult to climb but well worth the effort and fires in hearths should be kept burning if enthusiasm is to continue. Windows, representing the eyes of the soul, look out on backyards, pastures, parks and gardens, symbolizing that personal Garden of Eden which is by no means always an idyllic place. It represents the outside world, the dreamer's environment as he alone sees it. For some the flower beds are overgrown and weeds are taking over but for others an almost too orderly scene of regimentation suggests that even nature has been robbed and restrained! Who and what comes into this garden, either as welcome visitors or as unwanted intruders, is important for they represent friends and foes, uniquely but accurately disguised.

It took a dream using the mansion of the soul theme to help a man regain his pride and his self-confidence. In his dream he found himself standing at a garden gate which was half-off its hinges. The garden looked slightly overgrown but this was nothing compared with the delapidation of the outside of the house. The paint was peeling, the chimney was lop-sided and the windows looked dingy and dull. Once inside the house, however, he was surprised to find it was in a remarkably good state of repair. In the kitchen a meal was waiting and although the rest of the house made little impression on him, it was neat, clean and tidy.

The interpretation, even before the dreamer took his personal circumstances into account, was obvious. By standing at the gate of the mansion of his soul, he was taking a detailed objective view and saw himself as others saw him. The delapidated exterior of his dream mansion reflected his neglected personal appearance but the contrasting orderliness inside reassured him that his problem was only superficial. And food in the kitchen meant food for thought so by thinking about himself in a different way this dreamer was able to return to his former, smarter image and so regain his self-respect and confidence.

Water Themes

Water as an underlying theme represents states of emotions and feelings. From watching a babbling brook to experiencing near drowning in fearful raging torrents, the depths and dangers from psychological undercurrents found in ourselves, other people and in situations as a whole, are all thus symbolized. The depth, clearness, cloudiness and turbulence of the water reveal aspects of a problem, so if we weather a storm at sea we know we can overcome a trying time, but if still waters run deep and look murky into the bargain then we are being warned of unseen complications, not to mention possible cross currents.

The theme of a great inundation is a dream experienced by many and there are two possible interpretations of this. One is that it is a collective premonition of a natural disaster similar to the biblical Flood and the other is that it is purely personal, showing the dreamer that his life is on the point of being overpowered by a great wave of emotion. In these dreams the dreamer usually survives but many others are drowned.

Birth and Death Themes

To dream of a birth is said to mean a death and vice versa. Psychic dreamers often receive telepathic impressions from those about to be born into this world and from those about to depart, so they are well prepared for such events. Most dreams concerning babies, however, symbolize personal potential and hopes for the future for the dream-baby is the brainchild of the dreamer. Symbolically, this tells the dreamer that he has within all that is needed to achieve a lifelong ambition. The theme is the same, but the ambition is different.

Death as a dream theme, on the other hand, always leaves a worrying feeling behind. Although this is mainly a fear that the dream will turn out to be prophetic, as indeed it might, it is still a warning at the time of the dream. Even so it is sometimes impossible to avoid tragic consequences despite them having been spelled out clearly and in detail. Tragically, this is what the father of a weekend flyer discovered. In his dream he saw a light aircraft piloted by his son plough into the sea and although the dreamer begged him not to fly the next weekend the son insisted that dreams did not come true. By totally ignoring the warning message, this one did and so became prophetic and a premonition.

Mental Inoculation

When the inevitable happens following a dream warning it has, at least partially, prepared the dreamer for the shock, so in this respect it acts as an inoculation against mental trauma. Fortunately, most dreams concerning death are symbolic, pointing out that the 'victim' is facing a crisis in his or her life and needs all the help and understanding the dreamer can give. A friend's nightmare from years ago typifies this. When her daughter was seven years old she dreamed she saw her lying face downwards in a large drinking trough, as if drowned. She was wearing her striped school dress and her satchel was weighing her down. This is nearly twenty years ago so it is easy to see, in retrospect, just how symbolic it was, meaning the girl was weighed down with the pressures of school and all it entailed.

Knowing how the dreaming mind latches on to metaphors, it is hardly surprising that our dreams use the death theme as they do. 'I'll kill that so and so' may be said more in jest than in anger but it still makes an ideal model to be used at the appropriate time, so when someone displeases us, the 'I'll see them dead first' image is promptly taken out of storage and served up as a stiff dream message!

If the dead person is actually in a coffin it may be that we feel 'It is their funeral', meaning their troubles are all their own fault. But, depending on personal circumstances, it may mean that something like their love for us has died but we cannot bear to face the truth of this when we awake so have to be shown it in this way. To see oneself dead, even when a definite date is given, means we have a time limit to finish or complete something in life. The end of a phase is signified with the death of the old self and the birth, or rebirth, of a new us!

Nudity Themes

To wander down the road in a vest that is far too short, or even completely in the nude, may seem funny the next day but it was no joke when it happened most realistically in the dream. The nudity theme was once thought to indicate guilt feelings of a sexual nature but we now know that these scantily dressed experiences show that the dreamer fears another sort of exposure in public. He feels vulnerable and for all to be revealed would indeed be a disgrace. Clothes represent our outer façade, they are our different characteristics and our personality that usually protects and hides the real us inside. Remove these clothes and it is not the body, but the secret self that is bared.

On a more practical level nudity can simply be a warning that we are revealing too much of ourselves and giving away too many personal secrets. On forming a new friendship a lady dreamed that she met this friend and whilst talking to him noticed, to her horror, that articles of her clothing were vanishing one by one! When she was completely nude and thoroughly embarrassed she woke up. All had been revealed in this dream but hopefully it saved her from letting too many cats out of the bag at their next meeting which might have spoiled the relationship.

Journey Themes

The travelling theme is important although it often forms part of a much fuller dream. Whether this journey is made by train, boat, car, aeroplane, bike or by walking, it represents our destiny, our way through life. Railway stations, bus stops, airport terminals and petrol stations are all places where we halt and wait to decide in which direction we shall travel next. To miss a bus means we must not panic and although one opportunity has been missed, another, like the next bus, will soon come along. 'Be patient' is the message and remain confident in the future.

Help and Healing Themes

Help and healing in dreams takes many forms. Nightmares, for example, generally considered to be bad dreams, can be healing processes in themselves. Those associated with illness and fevers which produce a rapid increase of the body's metabolism, making us sweat and our hearts beat madly sending what seems like a surge of enormous energy through the system have amazing curative powers. After all, the key to all healing is energy and the following nightmare made national headlines in 1979 but it is only one of many similar experiences that go by unrecorded and even unrecognized.

Dream Cure For a Dog Lover

Widower George Edwards dreamed up an amazing cure for the brain tumour which paralysed the left side of his body. He awoke in his hospital bed with a start after a vivid nightmare and found he could move his left arm and leg again. Mr Edwards, a 64-year-old tyre fitter, was admitted to Ashford Hospital, Middlesex after doctors diagnosed the tumour. He was then transferred to London's Middlesex Hospital. There he dreamed that his sole companion, Rufus, the corgi, was to be put down. 'The nightmare was really vivid. I was convinced Rufus was going to be put down,' said Mr Edwards at his home in Middlesex. 'I woke up with a cry and a terrible jolt and a big shock went through my left arm and leg. The nurses were absolutely amazed when I got out of bed and lifted up a chair. The doctors said they had never known anything like it.' Six days after the nightmare he was well enough to go home. 'It was my corgi that cured me. In the dream I was convinced he was going to be killed and it shocked me back into action again,' says Mr Edwards.

To receive healing from our dreams all we have to do is to incubate a healing dream, although in Mr Edwards' case it was apparently spontaneous. Whilst it is true, therefore, that we do not necessarily have to do this to receive such help, to be on the safe side we can always ask for energy to be directed to that part of us that needs recharging and restoring whilst we sleep. If, however, we feel a more practical remedy is what we need, then by asking for this it will be revealed in its own unique way. These dreams do not have to be interpreted because their message is often brought to life and put into action in real life as a continuation of the dream itself. It is all part of that positive chain of action and reaction beginning with the request and incubation, as this next dream shows.

A Practical Dream Cure

The dreamer had suffered from a chronic but mild fever for over six months and nothing his doctor prescribed had any effect on this condition. Concentrating on this malady and making a suitable request to his dreaming mind for a remedy, the following dream was successfully incubated. In this the dreamer was walking past a shop and in the window he noticed a clear glass bottle labelled 'Tonic'. On waking he associated this rather unenthusiastically with his physical condition and decided if that was what his dream said, then a tonic from the chemist would do the trick. That morning on his way to the chemist the dreamer passed an off-licence and something in the window caught his eye. There, among the wines and spirits, were clear glass bottles labelled 'Tonic Water'. Instantly, his dream was broken. He went in and bought half a dozen bottles of tonic water, forgot all about the chemist's tonic, went home and drank them. That night, for the first time in months, he did not have a fever. What had happened was that the tonic water he drank contained quinine, a well-known treatment for malaria and some other febrile conditions. After a month on this the dreamer felt his fever had left him for good but he always keeps a bottle of his dream remedy handy, just in case.

Psychological Help

We can receive psychological help from ourselves through our dreams too if we really want it, but sometimes we may jib at this advice because it means swallowing our pride. When two friends fell out recently, a feud developed between them that was growing daily in intensity and this caused great emotional distress to one of them who could see no way out. Fortunately, she asked herself for a dream to try to solve the problem and this is what came after three requests on three successive nights. The dreamer was in her garden looking at dark storm clouds gathering overhead. In one corner of the garden under a tree was an axe so the dreamer went over and picked it up. As she did so it turned into a spade and with it she began to dig a hole. When she had done this she placed the axe-cum-spade in the hole and then filled it in with soil. The answer to her request was itself symbolic, namely burying the hatchet, which in turn had to be interpreted. As advice it made sense but whether she could or would act upon this is another matter.

Progression of Dreams

The long-term effect from a dream can be everlasting, as we have seen from the Pharoah's dream. By tracing the present world situation back to that event it becomes the cause from which most of mankind's collective destiny and history has since stemmed. Individually, our own dreams do much the same thing. Sometimes the continuum goes unnoticed but sometimes, like the man who recognized the bottles of tonic in the off-licence next day and the lady mentioned earlier who dreamed of an umbrella and remembered a romantic date, they are given credit for their powers. Who can say where the effect from any one dream will lead us?

If a particular dream impresses us, especially if there is a person in it whom we cannot identify as an aspect of ourselves or recognize as someone we know, then we can return to that dream situation when awake and not only have an action-replay but make that person reveal his identity. We created him in our dream so part of us, our dreaming mind, must know who or what that figure represents. To discover this we have to visualize the scene and re-enact it, consciously. When the unidentified figure comes into view we challenge him firmly and so discover whom or what he represents.

It is important, however, to remember that this figure may not be representing a person at all but a figment of our imagination brought in to convey a particular fear or problem. This, symbolized as a person, is exactly what we would expect the dreaming mind to do! Tradition uses a slightly bent-cloaked figure as the advance guard of death so here is one model for a start. We talk constantly of pathetic figures, angry people and miserable creatures to describe what we think are emotional and psychological states in others so why should these not enter our dreams exactly as we star them? The answer is that they do! Interpret the trait and we discover the person or state it symbolizes.

Forgiveness and a Murderer's Dream

One of the most impressive dreams I have ever tried to interpret came from a man who was serving a life sentence for murdering his wife during a fit of jealous rage. In his dream, which was repetitive over several months, he re-enacted the event and saw the terrible infliction in detail followed by the dying of his wife. Then, as he looked in horror at what he had done, the wound slowly healed, scarred over and then vanished. This was followed by the complete recovery of his wife. The obvious interpretation of this seemed to be that in his remorse he regretted what he had done and, as a wish-fulfilment dream, would like to be able to reverse his actions. Be that as it may, I do not think our dreaming minds are as naive as not to know we cannot go back in time and alter events once committed. There is, therefore, more to this dream than that.

Beginning as a literal action-replay, this dreamer relived the incident. The dream then went on to the symbolic recovery of his wife. This, I believe, meant that she had forgiven him for what he had done. Forgiveness of oneself is often impossible but with the help of a dream and those involved, dead or alive, it is perhaps possible to receive at least their forgiveness.

Dreams and Life

Dreams are about life and life is about dreams. It does not seem to matter how many mistakes we make, at our own expense of course, not other people's, so long as we learn from them. After all, if we knew certain things at the time we would not have done them, thus proving we needed the experience in the first place. Dreams, the greatest gift from ourselves to ourselves, will give us a short cut to that experience but only if we acknowledge them as sources of great power and enlightenment. We also have to accept that they are, in principle, the same for everyone. We all have prophetic dreams, warning dreams, fear dreams, sexy dreams, psychic dreams and a thousand and one other types of dreams varying in proportion and degree, depending on our way of life and our need of them. If we are content with our lot and do not ask profound cosmic questions then we will not receive profound dreams. There would be no point in them so our dreaming mind does not bother to even hint at such things. On the other hand, if we earnestly seek solutions to creative, unique work, as did Professor Kekule, Leonardo da Vinci and other wise men, then we too will receive from our dreams those original solutions for which we seek.

6

THE DICTIONARY OF
DREAM SIGNS AND SYMBOLS

'A skilful dream interpreter is he who has the faculty to observe resemblances,' said Aristotle. Resemblances in dreams are look-alike situations where one set of circumstances represents another similar in many ways to parables which convey the same message in different guises. Although dreams have a language of their own, they also make full use of words, phrases, puns and plays on words so once we realize what our dreaming mind is about and recognize those verbal resemblances, this aspect of dream interpretation becomes obvious.

A good example of this is the first word in this and most dream dictionaries: *Abandon*. It describes a situation where the dreamer is stranded, perhaps lost and alone and although the word Abandon does not actually appear in the dream script, this word clearly sums up the scene as a whole. In this case it warns literally of desertion or symbolically it points out that isolation is just what the dreamer needs to achieve independence and attain his goal in life. Only the dreamer, not the interpreter, can possibly know which of these messages is right for him and this can be discovered by applying them to personal circumstances and situations.

However extensive and comprehensive a dream dictionary is, it cannot possibly give the complete meaning of a dream. It cannot translate the language of dreams into everyday language because it is not simply a question of substituting one word with another as we do when translating, say, English into French. In this lies the difference between a translation and an interpretation. What a dream dictionary can do, however, is to give symbolic and literal meanings, plus their pun and metaphorical meanings, of those signs and symbols recognized in our dreams and listed as such in our dream diaries.

Literal meanings in dreams are usually metaphorical or completely literal in which case they are self-explicit. Handcuffs, for example, show that the dreamer's hands are tied in relation to a particular situation and there is not much they can do about it. Many symbolic meanings, on the other hand, have been passed down to us from antiquity originating from dream interpretations inscribed on Egyptian, Babylonian, Indian and Chinese monuments but others have been gathered through the ages as the human race increased its knowledge and widened its horizons. Symbolic significances arising from archetypal, psychological and social origins are also included in this dictionary with the latest additions being the aeroplane, the computer and UFOs.

For all this it is the personal meaning of each word that matters far more than any dream dictionary definition. Although the dreaming mind makes full use of every available prop, especially words we use every day, when it comes to the meaning of those words its first choice will always be the unique associations built up and stored by the individual from their own experiences linked with that word. This is what makes each of us see life in our own way and what makes each of our dreams original works of art.

Dream Signs and Symbols and Their Meanings

Abbreviations

Literal:	lit
Symbolic:	sym
Pun:	pun
Metaphorical:	met

A

Abandon	lit	Forsaken, isolated and cast-off.
	sym	Need for independence.

Abbey   sym   Mansion of the Soul. Protection, high ideals and strong beliefs.

Abdomen   lit   A health warning.
                   sym   Vulnerability. Act on gut feelings.

Abduction   sym   A warning. Plans carried out against the dreamer's will.

Abort   lit   A warning of a miscarriage.
                   sym   Hope for the future destroyed. A miscarriage of justice.

Abroad   sym   An unusual foreign experience. Travel likely.

Abundance   sym   Riches emotionally and psychically.

Abyss   sym   Depths of depression. A testing time.

Accident   lit   A warning of danger.

Accounts   lit   A warning of overspending.
                   sym   Account of credit or debit in life's bank account.

Ace   sym   A prize, win and success.

Ace of Clubs   Financial security.

Ace of Diamonds   Success with new ventures, career and business.

Ace of Hearts   Success in love and with friends.

Ace of Spades   A warning of an almost immovable obstacle.

Acorn   sym   Great potential for the future. Family linked.

Acrobat   sym   Difficulties will be overcome in a roundabout way.

Actor & Actress sym Beware of false characters.

Adam & Eve   sym   Physical and spiritual heritage.

		Most fortunate dream symbols indicating harmony.
Adultery	lit	Guilty feelings.
	sym	Contaminate.
Aeroplane	sym	High-flying ideals. A plane crash: ideals need earthing.
Africa	sym	An increase of status. Unknown potential.
Afternoon	lit	A specified time.
	sym	Middle age.
Air	sym	Inspiration.
Aisle	sym	Narrow choice.
	pun	Isle, isolation.
Alarm	lit	A warning sign.
Albatross	sym	A good omen for the future.
Alligator	sym	Dangerous opposition.
Almonds	sym	Bitterness. Also healing qualities.
Altar	sym	Self-sacrifice.
Ambassador	sym	Self-representation.
Amber	sym	Magnetic attraction.
America	sym	Duality, twin situations.
Amethyst	sym	Peace of mind.
Ammunition	sym	Dangerous evidence that supports or destroys a case.
Amulet	sym	A sign of protection.
Anagram	sym	Secret hidden meanings.
Ancestors	sym	Inherited characteristics.
Anchor	sym	Strong attachments to a person or place.

Angel	sym	A dream messenger.
Animals	sym	Basic human insticts. Fear of certain creatures indicates lack of self-understanding. See individual animals.
Antiques	sym	Forgotten but valuable hopes and ideals.
Anvil	sym	The forging of a friendship. Physical strength on the increase.
Ape	sym	A warning of regression either personally or as a situation.
Apples	sym	Healing potential. To eat an apple warns of future consequences and responsibility. A sexual appetite.
Apricots	sym	Good health and good fortune.
Aquamarine	sym	Eternal youth and lasting friendships.
Arch	sym	Unification at the top. Promotion and realization of ideals.
Archer	sym	A person who knows where he or she is going. Also a person born under the sign of Sagittarius.
Ark	sym	Safety and protection during difficult times ahead.
Arm	lit	A warning of too much physical effort.
	sym	Better times shortly due to one's own effort.
Army	sym	Opposition and lack of support.
Arrow	sym	Love smitten. The goal is in sight so take aim and go for it.
Artist	sym	The creative aspect of the dreamer.
Ascend	sym	Progress. The ability to rise above problems.

Ashes	sym	Memories from the past.
Asia	sym	Mystery and romance.
Asparagus	sym	There is forging ahead at the spearhead so keep up with the rest.
Ass	met	Beware of making an ass of yourself in public.
Asthma	lit	A health hazard.
	sym	Inhibited inspiration leading to frustration.
Astronomer	sym	Look ahead as far as possible.
Atoms	sym	Great detail of a structural situation will be revealed.
Attack	lit	A warning of bodily harm.
	sym	Psychic protection needed.
Attic	sym	High ideals. The top room in the mansion of the soul.
Auction	sym	Beware of swift disposal of friends and assets.
Audience	sym	A stage of credibility has been reached.
Aunt	sym	A feminine aspect of the self giving support.
Australia	sym	Youthfulness and untapped potential.
Automobile	sym	The ambitious driving force conveying the dreamer along his or her destinational highway.
Autumn	sym	It is time to make the most of things.
Avalanche	sym	A warning of being overcome by force of circumstances.
Avocado	sym	An increase of social activities.
Awaken	sym	To awaken in a dream means a self-awakening is imminent.

Axe	sym	Contention between friends and acquaintances.

B

Baby	sym	The dreamer's brainchild. Great potential for the future.
Badger	sym	Rewards will be reaped from personal effort.
	pun	Expect to be worried, badgered.
Baggage	sym	A journey shortly. Personal attributes. A difficult wife.
Baker	sym	All will turn out right in the end.
Balcony	sym	An elevated vantage point relating to a situation.
Ball	sym	The world.
Ballet	sym	Tiptoe carefully through a problem.
Banana	sym	Small consolation.
Bandage	sym	Physical protection needed.
Bank	sym	Physical and mental resources.
Bankruptcy	sym	Poor physical and mental resources. Lack of all energy.
Baptism	sym	A new start. Forgiveness.
Barbecue	sym	Limitless social occasions.
Barber	sym	Beware of rash action and consequent loss of energy.
Barefoot	sym	Tread lightly over a difficult problem.
Barge	sym	A smooth but boring journey.
	pun	Do not barge into others.

Barking	sym	A warning sign of approaching danger or trouble.
Barley	sym	A personal state of health is represented.
Barn	sym	A store for practical experience within the Mansion of the Soul.
Barrel	sym	Financial security.
Barrier	lit	An obvious obstacle.
	sym	An obstacle but not so obvious.
Basement	sym	The store place in the Mansion of the Soul for hidden fears and anxieties.
Basin	sym	A font and source of sustenance and rejuvenation.
Basket	sym	A receptacle of the mind which carries benevolence to others.
Bath	sym	Troubles will soon be washed away.
Battle	sym	Fight the good fight, defending not attacking.
Bazaar	sym	Unexpected good fortune.
Beach	sym	A balance between earth and water, the head and the heart.
Beads	sym	Social and personal success. Broken beads indicate broken promises.
Beans	sym	Increase of strength and wealth.
Bear	sym	Russia. Mother earth. An overpowering force.
Beard	sym	Strength of own convictions. Disguise.
Beasts	sym	Heraldic or mythological beasts represent archetypal forces.
Beaver	sym	Industry. Hard work with high rewards.
Bed	sym	Comfort and sex. A bed on fire

indicates marital trouble.

Bedroom	sym	Personal and secret matters.
Beehive	sym	Activity, action and communal work.
Bees	sym	Ancient symbol of royal succession. Fortunate sign.
Beetles	sym	Mystical influences.
Beetroots	sym	A healing thought and healing food.
Beggars	sym	Request forgiveness.
Behead	met	Beware of losing your head. Heart v. head situation.
	sym	Archetypal ritual. Strong Celtic messages from afar and from the dead.
Bells	sym	A warning sign. Joyous announcement.
Bereavement	sym	Regrets.
Berry	sym	Fruits of labour.
	pun	Forget the past, bury it.
Bet	sym	Take a chance but be prepared for failure.
Bewitched	sym	Under the domination of another.
Bible	sym	Look for the truth.
Bicycle	sym	Success from own physical effort. Working towards fulfilling one's destiny.
Binoculars	lit	Able to see the way ahead clearly.
Birds	sym	High-flying ideals. Inspiration and messages from afar and from the dead.
Birth	sym	A fresh start in life. Try again.
Birthday	sym	A time to celebrate and to remember.
Biscuits	sym	Sweet memories.

Bishop   sym   Pomp; respect tinged with fear.

Black   sym   Negative situations and moods. Depression. Nothingness.

Blackberries   sym   Setbacks. Associations with negative forces.

Blackbird   sym   A warning sign. Possessiveness over territory.

Blacksmith   sym   Physical strength. Messenger from the gods.

Blanket   sym   Smothering over-protection.

Blind   sym   Spiritually unaware.

Blood   sym   Psychic energy.

Blossom   sym   Happiness and contentment but not necessarily permanently.

Blue   sym   Spiritual energy and protection.
                    mct   Blue mood.

Boar   sym   A pigheaded person.

Boat   sym   Destiny over life's smooth or troubled waters.

Bones   sym   Basic principles.

Book   sym   Learn from the experience of others.

Boomerang   sym   Rebounding circumstances.

Bottle   sym   Limitations and inhibitions.
                    pun   Bottled-up feelings.

Bouquet   sym   An award.

Box   sym   Too self-contained. Restricted emotions.

Boy   sym   Youthfulness. Healing energy.

Bracelet   sym   Union and reunion.

Brambles	sym	Difficulties encountered.
Bread	sym	Food for thought. Bread of life. Share with others.
Breakfast	sym	Thanksgiving celebration.
Breast	sym	Bosom pals. Close relationship.
Breath	lit	Breathlessness warns of a health problem.
	sym	The life force.
Bride	sym	Uninitiated. Ultra-feminine concepts.
Bridge	sym	A linking factor.
Broom	sym	Good fortune and changes shortly.
Brother	sym	A masculine supporter.
Brown	sym	Financial luck.
	met	A brown study.
Bugs	sym	Annoyances and small inconveniences.
Buildings	sym	Mansions of the Soul. The whole person.
Bull	sym	An angry person. Brute force.
Bulldog	sym	Defence and protection.
Bullet	sym	A warning of verbal sniping.
Bull's-eye	sym	Take aim in life. A target to be reached.
Burglar	sym	A bad aspect of the self overshadowing better virtues.
Burn	sym	Self-inflicted trouble.
	met	Beware of burning your fingers.
Bus	sym	Destiny. Bus stops indicate resting periods and the need to consider in which direction to travel next.
Butcher	sym	Caution is needed when making new acquaintances.

Butter	sym	Do not be side-tracked with soft talk.
Butterflies	sym	Romance, happiness and interesting social engagements.
Buttons	sym	Use intelligence. A lost button warns of over-spending.

C

Cabbage	sym	Vegetating, marking time.
Cage	sym	Caged animals mean inhibitions. Restrictions.
Cake	sym	Sexual fulfilment.
	met	Have your cake and eat it.
Calendar	sym	Worries concerning future events.
Calf	sym	Eventual success.
Camel	sym	Unusual sight to be expected.
Camera	sym	Keep your secrets to yourself.
Canal	sym	Related to childbirth and delivery.
Canary	sym	A message of happiness within limits.
Cancer	lit	A fear of illness.
	sym	A person born under the sign of Cancer.
Candle	sym	A lighted candle indicates plenty of spirit. An unlit candle means a disappointment.
Cannibal	sym	Self-destruction.
Canoe	sym	Self-reliance is essential.
	met	Paddle your own canoe.
Canyon	sym	*See* Abyss.
Captain	sym	A rise in status but added responsibility.

Cards	sym	Playing cards represent the game of life. Postcards indicate a short message soon.
Carnations	sym	Rebirth as in reincarnation. A fresh start.
Carols	sym	A happy and prosperous year ahead.
Carpet	sym	Elevated consciousness.
	met	Beware of being on the carpet.
Castle	sym	The Mansion of the Soul.
	met	A man's home is his castle.
Cat	sym	The psychic senses.
	met	A black cat is very fortunate.
Cathedral	sym	High and lofty ideals.
Cattle	sym	Grazing cattle mean contentment. To drive cattle indicates the need for concerted effort in one direction only.
Cauliflower	sym	Improvement in family relationships soon.
Cave	sym	The unconscious mind. Introverted personality. Trapped by one's own reactions to life.
Cedar	sym	Celtic heritage.
Cellar	sym	Fear and dark thoughts. The basement in the Mansion of the Soul.
Cemetery	sym	All adversities will be conquered.
Chain	sym	A strong link.
Chair	sym	An empty chair indicates unseen influences. Sitting in a chair signifies future comfort.
Chameleon	sym	Beware! People and situations may not be what they seem.

Cherries   sym   Temptation in love.

Chess   sym   The power of the gods. The game of evolution.

Chest   sym   Treasure trove.

Chickens   sym   Ambitions curtailed and projects will be difficult to get off the ground.

Children   sym   Where there is life there is hope.

Chimney Sweep   sym   A wedding and a happy union.

China   sym   Crockery denotes that domestic arrangements need careful handling. The country of China represents Buddhism.

Choir   sym   Religious inspiration and support.

Christ   sym   Perfect peace of mind. Divine protection.

Christmas   sym   Relax and enjoy the present.

Church   sym   Faith, hope and charity. Mansion of the Soul.

Cigarettes   sym   Stop everything. Relaxation is needed.

Circus   sym   Beware of going in circles.

Cliff   sym   Danger and an obstacle.

Cloak   sym   Sign of protection.

Clock   sym   It is later than you think.

Clothes   sym   The personality, façade and the character shown to others.

Clover   met   You will soon be in clover.

Clown   sym   Take certain situations more seriously.

Coal   sym   A store of great potential energy and strength.

Coat	sym	Protection against the world.
Cobweb	sym	Look out for traps in life from which escape will be difficult.
	met	Blow away the cobwebs of the mind.
Cock	sym	If crowing, expect to be victorious. If cocks are fighting prepare for family rows.
Coffin	sym	There is no escape from a particular situation.
Coins	lit	Financial improvement shortly.
	sym	Wealth of experience will bring lasting benefit.
Colour	sym	Each colour represents a different form of energy.
Comet	sym	Beware of forthcoming trouble and misfortune.
Computer	sym	The brain.
Cooking	sym	Plans are already being made and put into operation.
Coral	sym	Take special care when travelling on water.
Corks	sym	Troubles will be well contained.
Corpse	sym	A lifeless person and hanger-on.
Cousin	sym	Help from the family or close friend.
Cow	sym	A bovine character.
Crab	sym	A warning of devious manoeuvring.
Cradle	sym	An empty cradle indicates unfulfilled desires. A baby in a cradle means future rewards.
Cripple	sym	Give support to whomsoever needs it.

Crocodile	sym	A warning of underhand bargaining.
Cross	lit	To be cross indicates anger and resentment.
	sym	Protection. Archetypal sign of Christianity and the four elements of the creation: earth, fire, air and water.
Crossroads	sym	An important decision must be made soon.
Crow	sym	The spirit of Britain. Celtic influence.
Crown	sym	Glory, success and recognition.
Crystal	sym	Mysticism and healing.
Cucumber	sym	Recovery from an illness.
Cup	sym	The font of life containing the waters of life.
Curate	sym	Self-healing power.
Curse	sym	Protection urgently needed.
Curtain	sym	An obstacle preventing far-seeing vision.

D

Daffodils	sym	Wales. Hope springs eternal.
Dagger	sym	Beware of treachery and verbal stabs in the back.
Daisy	sym	A sign of love and affection. Simple kindness.
Dam	sym	Blocked emotions.
Dance	sym	Prelude to love-making.
Dark	sym	You are being kept in the dark over something. Depression.

Daughter	sym	Feminine aspect of the self. Eternal youth.
Deaf	sym	Ignorance is bliss.
	met	None so deaf as those who do not wish to hear.
Death	sym	The end of a phase in life. Off with the old and on with the new.
Debt	sym	Karmic deficits. Pay up and make up quickly.
Deluge	sym	Beware of overpowering emotions.
Descending	sym	A lowering of standards. Delving into the past.
Devil	sym	Evil influences.
Diamonds	sym	The whole, many-faceted self.
Digestion	lit	A health warning.
	sym	Assimilation of energy. Food for thought needed.
Disease	sym	Dis-ease. Worries and troubles.
Ditch	sym	Barrier and protection.
	met	Ditch it, drop it.
Doctor	sym	An authoritative figure to turn to. The self-healer within.
Document	sym	Beware of unclear legalities.
Dog	sym	A friend. Also the top dog and the underdog within.
	met	A dog in the manger.
Dough	met	Money.
Dove	sym	A personal sacrifice needed. Peace of mind later.
Dragon	sym	Terrestrial energy. Archetypal earthly force.

Drawers sym Personal compartments of the mind. Tidy thoughts.

Drink sym Simple nourishment needed. Spiritual needs.

Drown sym Overcome by emotions and pressures of life.

Drug sym A warning of being misled and duped.

Drum sym A message needing careful understanding.

Drunk sym Intoxicated with one's own exuberance.

Dumb sym Do not let the cat out of the bag.

Dust sym The past is catching up fast.

E

Eagle sym Extreme ambitions and domination.

Earrings sym An unusual distinction will be bestowed upon the wearer.

Ears sym Listen for good news but ignore gossip.

Earth sym Elemental principle. Great mother comfort. The basic principles in life.

Earthquake sym A warning of disruption and change.

East sym Adopt a passive role. Relax.

Eating sym A desperate need for fulfilment and comfort. Food for thought.

Echo sym Do not imitate the antics, moods or opinions of others.

Eclipse sym Beware of overshadowing someone and vice versa.

Eels	sym	An excellent love-life is indicated.
Effigy	sym	Love, but do not idolize.
Eggs	sym	Financial improvement. Future hope.
	met	A nest egg.
Elbow	sym	Sleeping in a strange bed.
Electricity	sym	An energy surge.
Elephant	sym	The earthly aspect of the self.
	met	Memory. Elephants never forget.
Elevator	sym	A good sign if ascending but a bad one if descending.
Elf	sym	A spirit of nature. A dream messenger.
Embers	sym	Dying hope, ambitions and aims.
Embroidery	sym	Beware of gross exaggeration.
Emerald	sym	Use caution and respect. A powerful influence.
End of the World	sym	The fall of a personal empire.
Engine	sym	The core and driving force.
Entrails	sym	Divination and sorcery.
Envelope	sym	Sealed envelopes denote unseen dangers. Open envelopes mean the obvious will be revealed.
Equator	sym	A good balanced state. Also the waistline.
Evening	lit	A specified time.
	sym	Old age.
Evil	sym	Bad destructive influences.
Expedition	sym	Explore all possibilities. Leave no stone unturned.
Explosion	sym	Expect a sudden shock or surprise.

Eyes   sym   Windows of the soul. Psychic sight.

F

Fables   sym   Falsehoods.

Faces   lit   Hypnagogic impressions.
                  sym   Personalities.

Factory   sym   Mundane, repetitive thoughts.

Fairs   sym   Superficialities. Fleeting happiness and relief.

Fairy   sym   Nature's dream messenger.

Falcon   sym   Beware of an enemy.

Falling   lit   Stage 1 sleep state.
                  sym   Insecurity. Fear of not attaining a goal.

Famine   sym   Prepare for hard times in the future.

Farm   sym   The domestic scene.

Fasting   sym   A health warning.

Father   lit   Father.
                  sym   Authoritative, masculine principles.

Feast   sym   Give thanks for what you have.

Feathers   sym   The good things in life.

Feet   sym   Foundations and balance in life.

Fence   sym   Know your limitations.

Ferns   sym   Natural remedies and Mother Nature.

Ferret   sym   Protect against viciousness.

Ferry   sym   Do not let others do too much for you.

Fields   sym   Back to nature and the simple things in life.

Figs	sym	Embarrassing things in life.
Film	sym	Action-replay of the past.
Fingers	sym	Dexterous.
Fire	sym	Elemental principle. Passions and emotions.
Fireworks	sym	Excitement followed by disappointment.
Fish	sym	Christianity. Sustenance for the soul.
Flag	sym	Patriotism. United, community spirit.
Flames	sym	Uncontrolled passion and emotions.
Fleece	sym	Disguised personality.
	pun	Beware of being fleeced.
Flies	sym	Worries caused by supposed friends.
Flood	sym	Beware of being overcome by emotions.
Flowers	sym	Individual fulfilment. Blossoming potential.
Flute	sym	The pipe of Pan. Magic vibration.
Flying	sym	Astral projection. Ability to rise above earthly problems.
Font	sym	Source of resuscitation.
Food	sym	Spiritual sustenance.
Fool	met	Do not be fooled.
Footsteps	sym	Someone is taking steps to investigate.
Foreign Land	sym	An unusual foreign experience is to be expected.
Forge	sym	Permanency.
Fossil	pun	An aged or old-fashioned person.

Fountain	sym	Waters of life. Healing and youthfulness.
Freemason	sym	Unrecognized friends from afar.
Friend	sym	Support in times of need.
Frog	sym	Transformation of character.
Fruit	sym	Rewards from hard work.
Funeral	sym	The end of a phase in life.
	met	It is their funeral.
Furniture	sym	Material possessions and comfort.

G

Gaiters	sym	An excellent sign for those in love.
Gale	sym	Better times ahead. Troubles will blow over.
Galloping	sym	Expect an increase in the pace of life.
Gambling	sym	It is the right time to take a chance.
Games	sym	Experiences in living. Exercises in sportsmanship.
Garage	sym	Protection and care taken to ensure destiny continues on the right road.
Garden	sym	Individual environment. The personal Garden of Eden.
Gargoyles	sym	Psychic guardians.
Garlic	sym	Protection from physical illness.
Gate	sym	The entrance to other dimensions.
Gems	sym	Mixed blessings.
Germs	sym	Invasion of private rights.
Ghost	sym	The spirit of a person.

Giant	sym	An overpowering personality. Feelings of inferiority.
Ginger	sym	Spice of life.
Giraffe	sym	Do not be inquisitive.
Girl	sym	Feminine, youthful aspect of the self.
Glass	sym	Celtic influence.
Gloves	sym	Security tinged with deviousness.
Gnome	sym	An earth elemental. Protector of the home and personal property.
Goat	sym	Know your friends and your enemies.
	met	Sort the sheep from the goats.
God	sym	A personal concept of the Creator.
Godparents	sym	Protection and benevolence.
Gold	sym	Sign of perfection.
Golf	sym	The solo game of life. Handicaps.
Goose	sym	Assets and capital.
	pun	Do not be a goose.
Gooseberry	sym	Two is company, three is a crowd.
Gospel	sym	God's spell. The truth is sought.
Grain	sym	Rewards reaped from one's own harvest.
Grapefruit	sym	The need of health-giving food and physical purification.
Grapes	sym	Affluence and plenty.
Grass	sym	Basic principles.
Grasshopper	sym	Do not jump to conclusions.
Grave	sym	Beware of emotional submission.
Gravestone	sym	Self-appraisal.

Greece	sym	Myth and mystery.
Green	sym	Serenity and balanced thinking.
Greyhound	sym	Keep the imagination under control and on a tight leash.
Grin	sym	You cannot get away with it!
Grow	sym	An increase in status generally.
Guest	met	You may be entertaining angels unawares.
Guitar	sym	Take care of the heart-strings.
Gypsy	sym	Show respect for unknown qualities and quantities.

H

Haddock	sym	Good fortune.
Haemorrhage	sym	Loss of energy.
Haggis	sym	A positive Scottish influence.
Hair	sym	Sexual powers.
Hall	sym	Communal feelings.
Halo	sym	Personal energy field. The aura.
Ham	pun	A bore/boar.
Hammer	sym	Drive home your point.
Hand	sym	The hand of God. Fate.
Handbag	lit	Personal possessions.
	sym	Private thoughts and opinions.
Handcuffs	sym	Your hands are tied.
Hand-grenade	sym	A warning of a dangerous and explosive situation.

Handkerchief	sym	Goodbye and sadness.
Hanging	sym	Loneliness.
Harbour	sym	Shelter from life's stormy sea.
Hare	sym	A mystical trail.
Harp	sym	A Welsh influence. Harmony.
Harvest	sym	Triumph and success in the end.
Hat	sym	Recognition and status symbol.
Hawthorn	sym	The god Bran.
Hay	sym	Success in your love-life.
Head	sym	Intellect, logic and knowledge.
Heart	sym	Love, intuition, inspiration and wisdom.
Hearth	sym	The home.
Heather	sym	Well-earned good fortune.
Heaven	sym	The heart's desire.
Hedge	sym	Barriers and limitations.
Height	sym	Life must be viewed from an elevated standpoint.
Helicopter	sym	Practical ideals and ambitions.
Hell	sym	A miserable outlook.
Helmet	sym	Teutonic influence.
Hen	sym	A black hen means personal sacrifice. A white hen means success. (*See* Chicken.)
Herbs	sym	Help and healing needed.
Herd	sym	Be individualistic.
Hermit	sym	Keep yourself to yourself more.
Heron	sym	Traditional inscriptions. Hieroglyphs.

Hill	sym	A goal or ambition to be attained.
Hippopotamus	sym	Heavy emotional influence.
Hit	sym	Beware of a quick temper.
Hive	sym	Industry, prosperity and security.
Hole	sym	An unseen trap.
Holiday	sym	Self-praise is justified.
Holly	sym	Holy, religious influence.
Home	sym	Feminine, maternal comforts.
Honey	sym	Sweetness and love.
Hood	sym	Death.
Hoof	sym	Beware of cheats and liars.
Hook	sym	Stop angling for compliments. A danger sign.
Horn	sym	Sexual prowess and desires.
Horse	sym	Energy drive. Horsepower.
Horseshoe	sym	Symbol of the Moon goddess. Good luck.
Hospital	sym	Hospice and hospitality. Rest is needed.
Hot	sym	Excess energy needs re-directing.
Hotel	sym	Loss of personal identity.
Hound	sym	Over-dog or under-dog. Dominant complexes.
House	sym	Mansion of the Soul.
Hunchback	sym	Better times ahead.
Hunger	sym	The urgent need to understand. Lack of satisfaction.
Hurricane	sym	Turmoil and upheaval.

Hut	sym	Simple single-mindedness.
Hymn Singing	sym	A divine message.

I

Ice	sym	Total lack of emotional feeling.
Iceberg	sym	Beware of what lies beneath the surface.
Icicles	sym	Anxieties will soon melt away.
Icon	sym	Sacred image of someone.
Idol	sym	Place no one on a pedestal.
Illness	lit	Beware of ill health.
Imposter	sym	Be true to yourself.
Impotence	sym	Powerless and helpless.
Incense	sym	Increase of sensitivity.
Incest	sym	Unhealthy emotional relationship.
Injury	sym	Protect against verbal attack.
Ink	sym	Writing in ink means state your case clearly. An ink blot means trouble caused by yourself.
Inoculation	sym	Initiations and experiences in life.
Insects	sym	Small annoyances.
Intestines	lit	Digestive trouble.
	sym	Worry.
Invisibility	sym	Unseen possibilities.
Iris	sym	The flower representing the goddess Iris, messenger of the gods.

Iron	sym	Strength and endurance. Will-power.
Island	sym	Isolation and pride.
Ivory	sym	Refinement but beware of isolation.
Ivy	sym	An emotional hanger-on.

J

Jade	sym	Do not rely on the opinion of others.
Jasmine	sym	Feminine qualities.
Jay	sym	Messenger from the dead.
Jerusalem	sym	Eternal hope.
Jesus	sym	Divine blessing and protection.
Jet	sym	Hard times are indicated by this black stone.
Jewels	sym	Riches of the mind.
Jockey	sym	A very fast mover.
Joker	sym	Be not deceived by naive behaviour.
Journey	lit	Travel and change.
	sym	Destiny.
Judge	sym	Do not pre-judge situations nor judge others.
Jug	sym	Life holds many more surprises.
Juggler	sym	Rearrange plans.
Jump	sym	Lack of continuity.
Junk	sym	Perish inane thoughts.
Jury	sym	The majority is always wrong.

K

Kangaroo	sym	Elusive, restless person.
Kennel	lit	The dog house.
	sym	Tied to the home.
Kettle	sym	Trouble brewing up on the home front.
Key	sym	Clue to a problem.
Kill	sym	Annihilation of an unacceptable characteristic of the self.
King	sym	Protector, guardian and highest masculine principle.
Kingfisher	sym	A change is to be expected soon.
Kiss	sym	Singled out for a special purpose.
Kitchen	sym	The domestic scene.
Kite	sym	Success will eventually come easily.
Kitten	sym	Potential ambition.
Knee	sym	A meeting with an important person.
Kneel	sym	Have respect for others.
Knife	sym	To be stabbed with this indicates enemies.
Knight	sym	Chivalry.
Knit	sym	Union.
Knock	sym	Be on the alert.
Knot	sym	Difficult and tangled emotions need unravelling.

L

Labyrinth	sym	It is essential to solve a certain mystery.

Lace	sym	A secret love.
Ladder	sym	The connection between the conscious and unconscious minds.
Ladybird	sym	Success in a small way.
Lake	sym	Smooth sailing and easier times ahead.
Lamb	sym	Initiation into esoteric mysteries.
Lame	sym	Slow progress due to obstacles.
Land	sym	The environment.
Lantern	sym	A hanging lantern is a warning sign otherwise it is a welcome one.
Larder	sym	Emotional and mental reserves.
Laughter	sym	Laugh only at yourself.
Laundry	sym	A fresh and clean start.
Lawn	sym	Cultivate a calm nature.
Lawyer	sym	Seek professional advice.
Leaf	sym	When on a tree life will prosper but if on the ground hardship is likely.
Leather	sym	An unfortunate, materialistic sign.
Lecture	sym	Expect to be spoken down to.
Leek	sym	Like onions, a leek is a sign of good health. A symbol of Wales.
Letter	sym	Unexpected news.
Lettuce	sym	Problems will be fleeting and seasonal.
Lice	sym	Take greater care with personal presentation.
Lift	sym	Ascending means inspired thoughts. Descending means not depression but coming down to earth.

Light   sym   Spiritual energy. The right way ahead.

Lighthouse   sym   A Mansion of the Soul able to withstand the roughest of life's storms.

Lily   sym   The sign of the Holy Family.

Lion   sym   A brave and strong person.

Lizard   sym   Someone may appear to be dangerous but they are not.

Lobster   sym   Bashfulness will be overcome.

Lock   sym   Unless a key is in the lock it means you face an obstacle.

Looking Glass sym   Reflections from the past.

Lost   sym   Insecurity, uncertainty and no plans have been made for the future.

Luggage   sym   Superficial personal qualities which can hamper progress.

Lynx   sym   A quick-witted, skilful person.

M

Maggot   sym   Great changes are to be expected.

Magnet   sym   Sex appeal and personal attractiveness.

Magpie   sym   A black and white, yes and no situation.

Man   sym   In a woman's dream he represents her animus. In a man's dream he is an undefined aspect of himself.

Mansion   sym   The whole person, body, mind and spirit.

Manure   sym   Recycling of energy. Wealth and plenty.

Map	sym	Fate and the future is at stake.
Marble	sym	Monuments to the past.
Marigold	sym	The symbol of the Mother Goddess.
Market	sym	Choose carefully but a choice must be made.
Marriage	lit	A wedding.
	sym	Union of opposites. Mystical marriage.
Marsh	sym	Unseen difficulties and dangers.
Martyr	sym	Self-sacrifice, self-destruction.
Mask	sym	Beware of deception and deceit.
Mass	sym	Healing and an increase of energy.
Mast	sym	A sign of direction and forthcoming journeys.
Mat	sym	Be discerning when discussing the affairs of others.
Maze	sym	The pattern of many incarnations.
Meat	sym	To eat meat indicates a basic need is lacking in life. To cook it for others shows generosity.
Medicine	sym	Retribution.
Medium	sym	A dream messenger.
Melon	sym	Events will take a turn for the better.
Mermaid	sym	A water elemental. A symbol of an unobtainable lover.
Metal	sym	The kingdom of the earth and of the gnomes.
Meteor	sym	A strong warning sign.
Microscope	sym	Discoveries will be made but they will be insignificant.

Milk   sym   Human kindness and support.

Mill   sym   Water and windmills indicate a peaceful life later on.

Mint   sym   Recovery of health.

Mirror   sym   The answer lies in reversing the situation and role in life. Memories.

Miser   sym   A mean personal characteristic.

Mistletoe   sym   Show respect for a potentially dangerous situation.

Mole   sym   Keep out of the way until the danger passes.

Money   lit   Financial matters generally.
                sym   Wisdom and knowledge.

Monk   sym   A dream messenger. The altruistic self.

Monkey   sym   A devious but amusing character.

Moon   sym   Keep control over emotions. Power over the mind.

Morning   sym   Youthfulness.

Moss   sym   External healing forces should be investigated.

Moth   sym   Happiness at night.

Mother   lit   Mother.
                sym   Maternal instincts, protection and compassion. The great mother. Feminine domination.

Mother-in-Law lit   Mother-in-law.
                   sym   A force to be reckoned with. An unknown quantity.

Motor Cycle   sym   Destiny. Life is speeding up considerably.

Mountain	sym	An aim in life which is not easily attained.
Mouse	sym	Lie low and play the inferior role for a time.
Move	lit	A move to a new abode.
	sym	Take steps to bring about a necessary change in life.
Mud	sym	The elements of earth and water, practical and emotional characteristics. Mixed blessings.
Museum	sym	Old memories and old friends.
Mushrooms	sym	Mystical connections.
Music	sym	Harmonious music links the body with the soul. Disruptive music destroys the peace of mind.
Mustard	sym	Nothing is impossible.

N

Nail	sym	This plus effort means achievement. A warning of outside interference.
Naked	sym	Guilty feelings. The bare truth.
Narrow	sym	There is no choice but to continue.
Neck	sym	Do not take risks.
Needle	sym	Continue with attempts to make amends.
Negro	sym	Richness and colour will soon be added to life.
Neighbour	sym	Oneself.
Nest	lit	The home.
	sym	Protection from the big bad world.

Net	sym	An obvious trap exists so beware.
New Year	sym	Rebirth. A new beginning with lots of hope for the future.
Niece	sym	Feminine family support.
Night	sym	A time to take it easy, give up and rest.
Nightingale	sym	Love and romance is in the air.
North	sym	Norse god. Teutonic influence.
Nose	sym	Friends will rally round if needed.
Numbers	sym	Dates, anniversaries and future and past events.
Nun	sym	Compassion and self-denial.
Nurse	sym	Self-help and self-healing is needed.
Nut	sym	Tremendous potential for the future.
Nymph	sym	A nature spirit and dream messenger.

O

Oak	sym	A strong heart. Druidic influence.
Oar	sym	Personal effort and guidance.
Oats	sym	Sexual appetite.
Observatory	sym	Look far beyond the present situation for an answer.
Ocean	sym	Vast emotional potential, good and bad.
Office	sym	The filing room of the memory in the Mansion of the Soul.
Officer	sym	Expect respect and an increase of official status.

Ogre	sym	An unreasonable fear, pantomime fashion.
Oil	met	Pour oil on troubled waters.
	sym	Do not mix two principles or standpoints.
Ointment	sym	Healing balm.
Old Man	sym	The experienced, wise self within.
Old Woman	sym	The intuitive, compassionate self within.
Olives	sym	The Holy Land.
Onions	sym	Health-giving influences and surrounding protection.
Opal	sym	A warning of unfortunate circumstances.
Operation	sym	Interference and invasion of privacy.
Opium	sym	Beware of being duped into submission.
Orange	sym	Sunshine, cheerfulness and good health.
Orchard	sym	The Garden of Eden. Temptation and excesses.
Orchestra	sym	Keep in tune with those around you.
Orchids	sym	Passionate love.
Organ	sym	Religious influences.
Ornament	sym	False standards.
Ostrich	met	Beware of burying your head in the sand.
Owl	sym	Feminine wisdom, white witches and the goddess Athene.
Oxen	sym	Mundane and earthy natured.

| Oxygen | sym | Inspired thoughts. Vitality. |
| Oyster | sym | The world. |

P

Pain	lit	A warning of physical pain and problems.
	sym	Emotional agony.
Parachute	sym	An escape is possible but this could be dangerous.
Parcel	sym	A surprise.
Parents	sym	Inherited attributes and inferior qualities.
Parrot	sym	Repeated, worthless gossip.
Parsley	sym	Feminine dominance.
Party	sym	Avoid certain organizations and groups.
Path	sym	Destiny and path through life.
Pattern	sym	The treadmill of life.
Peach	sym	Bitter-sweet memories.
Peacock	sym	A warning sign. Beware of strutting boasters.
Pearls	sym	Tears of the Moon goddess. Sadness.
Peas	sym	A difficult choice will have to be made soon.
Pen	sym	Sexual happiness.
	met	The pen is mightier than the sword.
Pencil	sym	Stealth, wealth and health.
Penguin	sym	Difficulties will be encountered.

Perfume	sym	A manifestation through the sense of smell.
Photograph	sym	Comparisons and memories should be kept secret.
Piano	sym	A means of communication.
Picture	sym	A literal or symbolic message.
Pig	sym	A disrespected person.
Pigeon	sym	Town and country atmosphere.
Pillars	sym	Support will be given.
Pine Trees	sym	Celtic oracle.
Planets	sym	The sky is the limit. Ambitions, aims and goals are all attainable.
Plants	sym	Life itself. Barometers of health and environment.
Plastic	sym	Artificial emotions. Brittle thoughts.
Plough	sym	Patience will be rewarded.
Plum	sym	The right choice will be made. Improvement soon.
Police	sym	Authority, law and order.
Pond	sym	Happy feelings and emotions.
Potatoes	sym	Earthy responses to earthy problems.
Powder	sym	Beware of undermined confidences.
Prayer	sym	Help is on the way.
Pregnant	sym	Ideas have been conceived but only time will tell if they will succeed.
Primrose	sym	Love-affairs need careful handling.
Prison	sym	Self-made rules and restrictions bring inhibitions.

Puppet   sym   A warning that someone is dominating the scene.

Pyramid   lit   Egyptian influence.
    sym   Start at the bottom and work up from there to the top.

Python   sym   Sign of Pythia, a Greek priestess and dream messenger.

Q

Quarry   sym   Make every effort to discover the truth.
    met   The truth lies in a stone.

Quartet   sym   The fourfold nature of life. The four elements.

Quay   sym   Make the most of the calm before the storm.

Queen   sym   The superior mother. The goddess Venus.

Queue   sym   Patience is a virtue.

Quicksand   sym   Beware! Danger ahead.

Quoits   sym   The skilful game of loving and living.

R

Rabbi   sym   Old Testament influence. Judaic message.

Race   sym   The pace of life. Also rivalry.

Radio   sym   External influences. Telepathic messages.

Raft   sym   Beware of isolation and drifting into troubled waters.

Rags	sym	Poor circumstances can be improved with effort.
Railway	sym	The speed of life. The destinational route.
Railway Stations	sym	Stop and think well before continuing on the present course.
Rain	sym	The washing away of fears, anxieties and worries. A refreshing sign.
Rainbow	sym	The seven colours denote different healing energies.
Ram	sym	Patriarchal dominance.
Rape	sym	Avoid all who cause the slightest fear or worry.
Raven	sym	The crow. Bran and the spirit of Britain.
Recipe	sym	Prescription for good health.
Red	sym	Basic energy drives including sex, ambition, anger and physical healing.
Red Cross	sym	Healing sign.
Reptile	sym	Nasty but unfortunate person.
Reservoir	sym	Store of personal energy. The psychic battery.
Restaurant	sym	Food and sustenance are needed for mind and spirit.
Revolving Door	sym	Opportunities have been missed in the past.
Rhinoceros	sym	Traditionally a sex symbol. Good protection, too.
Rhyme	sym	The rhythm of life holds the secret.
Rice	sym	Good news on the domestic scene.

Riding	sym	Riding any animal means the mastery and conquest of a person, a talent or a handicap.
Ring	sym	A long unbroken friendship. Marriage and engagement.
River	sym	The flowing of the waters of life. Destiny.
Road	sym	The road through life with all that is encountered along the way.
Robber	sym	Fear and insecurity.
Robin	sym	A message from a loved one now departed.
Romance	sym	Love and romance will soon blossom again.
Room	sym	One particular aspect of a person. One room in the Mansion of the Soul.
Root	sym	Stability, confidence and strength.
Rope	sym	Strong attachment to a person or place.
Rosemary	sym	Remembrances.
Roses	sym	Messages of love.
Row	sym	Rowing on water shows a concerted effort has been made to complete a project or phase in life.
Royalty	sym	Personal association with royalty indicates an understanding of natural forces and the part each individual plays in the scheme of things.
Running	sym	Stop! Face the truth.

S

Sack	sym	The future has yet to be revealed.
Sacrifice	sym	Make a personal sacrifice.
Saddle	sym	Beware of binding commitments.
Sage	sym	Healing thoughts.
Sailor	sym	A fortunate sign bringing changes for the better.
Saint	sym	Guardian angel and protector.
Salad	sym	Back to nature and simplicity. Avoid complexities.
Sale	sym	An increase of wealth provided bread is cast onto the waters of life.
Salmon	sym	The sacred fish of the Celts.
Salt	sym	The element earth.
Sand	sym	Annoyances and inconveniences but not lasting.
Sapphires	sym	Use restraint, discretion and decorum.
Satellite	sym	Watch out for those on the periphery.
Saw	sym	Sawing wood cuts one down to size.
Scar	sym	An emotional wound from the past that is healed but not forgotten.
Scent	sym	A psychic manifestation through the sense of smell.
School	sym	The school of life with all its lessons to be learned.
Scientists	sym	Let the heart rule as well as the head.
Scissors	sym	Cut any unnecessary ties and links.
Sea	sym	*See* Ocean.

Seeds	sym	Great things can grow from small beginnings provided they are sown at the right time.
Sewing	sym	Make do with what is available at present.
Sex	lit	A wishful thinking sign.
	sym	A decoy or cover-up for a guilty pursuit.
Shadow	sym	The latent possibility of the individual.
Shapes	sym	The language of the mind.
Sheep	sym	Be individualistic and be true to yourself.
Shepherd	sym	The guardian of the spirit.
Ship	sym	The whole self when life is uncertain and all at sea.
Shoes	sym	Steps to take and those taken already in life.
Shop	sym	Choice and difficult decisions. Selling ideas to others.
Signature	sym	All will be revealed and there will be no mystery.
Silk	sym	Riches and luxury. Chinese influence.
Silver	sym	Make the best of second best!
Singing	sym	Collective message bringing good news. Troubles are passing.
Sister	sym	The feminine aspect generally.
Skeleton	sym	Look for the cause and do not be put off by the effects.
Sky	sym	Heaven. There are no limitations to success.

Sledge   sym   A quick reaction but control is lacking.

Slide   sym   Things are getting out of control.

Smile   sym   This could be a superficial sign but only time will tell.

Smoke   sym   A message warning of danger and trouble.

Snakes   sym   These represent physical, psychic and spiritual energy in the forms of sexual drive, ambitions, emotions – good and bad – and healing.

Snow   sym   Cleansing and purity.

Soldiers   sym   War within and war without. Beware!

South   sym   Gods of the south. The prime of life and happiness.

Sparrow   sym   A cockney person or Londoner.

Spell   sym   Bad influences from someone or somewhere.

Spider   sym   The overwhelming female figure. Also industriousness at a price.

Spirit   sym   A ghost from the past, memory or manifestation of a dead person.

Spoon   sym   Self-help and self-pampering is needed.

Spring   sym   Fresh hope will spring up suddenly.

Square   sym   Stability and four-square support.

Stag   sym   A bachelor.

Stage   sym   The stage of life. Personal appearance as seen by others.

Stairs   sym   Ascending indicates a rise in status, success and acclaim but descending means loss of recognition and confidence.

Star	sym	A birth.
Statue	sym	Frozen feelings and emotions.
Steal	sym	Make amends and pay up before it is too late.
Steel	sym	Nature plus man's ingenuity will solve a problem.
Stones	sym	Possessions of the gnomes! Leave well alone. Do not disturb the course of nature.
Stork	sym	A new arrival.
Straw	sym	Comfort is essential if an aim is to be accomplished.
Suffocation	sym	A health warning sign.
Suicide	sym	Self-guilt, self-persecution and self-destruction.
Sun	sym	God's gift to mankind. The source from which flows sustenance and support.
Sunflower	sym	An old, welcome friend.
Swan	sym	The sign of the White Goddess.
Swastika	sym	An ancient symbol of power.
Sweep	sym	Start off right or the project will fail. Make a clean sweep first.
Sweets	sym	Lovers and admirers of the opposite sex.
Swim	sym	Life is a struggle but it can be overcome if you do not swim against the stream.
Sword	sym	A sign of defence and attack.

T

Table	sym	An altar upon which lie beliefs, achievements and hopes.
Tap	sym	To hear a tap means an important contact has been made.
Tarantula	sym	Beware of being your own worst enemy.
Taxi	sym	Take advantage of all available help even though it may cost money.
Tea	sym	Innocent friendship, at least at present.
Teacher	sym	Self-reliance and the guru within.
Tears	sym	The dividing line between happiness and sadness is thin.
Teeth	sym	Stages in life that are associated with changes from babyhood to old age.
Telephone	sym	Listen to others but do not necessarily accept their advice.
Telescope	sym	Far-seeing but all is still not clear nor has been revealed.
Television	sym	A repeat performance of certain aspects in life.
Temple	sym	A private retreat where dreams are made.
Thread	sym	Fate and karma.
Thunder	sym	The warning voice of the gods.
Tide	sym	The ebbing and flowing of emotions and feelings tied to external events.
Tiger	sym	Get up and go energy.
Toad	sym	The philosopher and his magic stone.

Toilets sym Basic needs in life. Gut feelings and the elimination of unwanted experiences and memories.

Tomb sym Terrible restrictions which should be removed quickly.

Tower sym Towering ambitions which could isolate and become unrealistic.

Train sym The collective and individual journey through life. Travelling between stages and events.

Treasure sym Unique inventions and original ideas.

Trees sym Family matters generally.

Triangle sym Stability and protection.

Tunnel sym The present is limited and cramped but there is light at the end of the tunnel.

Turkey sym Those who make the most noise know the least.

Turtle sym An oracle. Coincidences will reveal the right answer.

Twins sym Dual aspects and two sides of a problem must be considered.

Typewriter sym Speed up communications with those who need help.

U

UFO sym The individual search for the Holy Grail. Personal psychic potential.

Umbrella sym Take shelter from life with all its storms.

Uncle	sym	A reliable and experienced friend in time of need.
Undertaker	sym	Undertake an unpleasant job yourself.
Undressed	sym	Personal secrets could be revealed unless care is taken to cover them up.
Unhappy	sym	A deep-seated fear which needs to be expressed.
Unicorn	sym	A source of purity, a sign of virginity and a symbol of altruistic beliefs.
Uniform	sym	A respect for authority albeit unfounded.
Universities	sym	Ancient centres of learning in the western tradition.
Urine	sym	An expression of relief after a tense time.
Urn	sym	Ashes to ashes and dust to dust. Reincarnation of a spirit into a family is due.

V

Vaccination	sym	Emotional protection against adversary.
Valley	sym	There is little choice at present but at least the way is straight albeit narrow.
Vampire	sym	A person who exhausts and drains others of vitality.
Vegetables	sym	Basic necessities which are all too easily overlooked.
Veil	sym	The truth is there but it requires uncovering.
Velvet	sym	Beware of what lies beneath the surface.

	met	Beware too of the iron fist in a velvet glove.
Venison	sym	Someone is getting above their station in life!
Ventriloquist	sym	Investigate thoroughly certain sources of information.
Vest	sym	Lack of confidence fails to conceal personal secrets.
Vicar	sym	A sign of orthodox religion.
Village	sym	Good foundations exist but this is only a beginning.
Vine	sym	Spiritual inheritance.
Vinegar	sym	Be not deceived. It is all for the good.
Violets	sym	Flowers of the spirit.
Violin	sym	Emotional harmony can confidently be expected.
Viper	sym	Misplaced energies. A dangerous person is around.
Volcano	sym	An explosion of emotions is to be expected at any time.
Vomit	sym	An unpleasant cause will vanish soon.
Voyage	sym	Travel abroad is likely. Life's voyage into the future will be more peaceful.
Vulture	sym	A vicious competitor is waiting to move in and take his or her pick.

W

| **Waiter** | sym | Be of service to others. |

Walking   sym   Rewards will be reaped through personal efforts. Destiny will continue at a slow but sure pace.

Wall   sym   An obstacle which prevents a satisfactory view of true circumstances.

Wallet   sym   The masculine version of the handbag. Personal beliefs and thoughts which are private.

Wallflowers   sym   The odd one out.

Walnuts   sym   Well provided for but no luxuries.

War   sym   Conflict and aggression.

Wash   sym   Forget the past and begin again. All is forgiven.

Wasp   sym   A warning of enemies close at hand.

Watch   sym   Time marches on. Do not waste a minute.

Water   sym   The unconscious self. Heartfelt emotions. The waters of life.

Wealth   sym   Wisdom accumulated from experience.

Weaving   sym   The pattern of life woven in time and space.

Web   sym   Beware of a trap from which escape will be virtually impossible.

Wedding   lit   A wedding.
    sym   Union of the conscious and unconscious minds.

Well   sym   Depth of feeling. Source of inspiration.

West   sym   Atlantis and hope for mankind.

Whale   sym   The feminine self. The womb of Mother Nature.

Wheat	sym	Fertility and plenty.
Wheel	sym	A warning of going in circles. Time.
Whistle	sym	A warning giving time to avert trouble.
White	sym	Spiritual awareness. A combination of all the healing colours.
Whitewash	sym	Disguise and cover-up.
Willow	sym	Family problems associated with temporary sadness and disappointment.
Wind	sym	The element air. Beware of indiscretions and gossip.
Window	sym	The outlook for the future. The eyes of the soul.
Wine	sym	Good health, happiness and prosperity.
Winter	sym	A quiet, resting time.
Witch	sym	Disenchantment with people and conditions.
Wolf	sym	Beware of hard times.
Woods	sym	Do not let details obscure the main objective.
Wool	sym	Protection against verbal blows in this world.
World	sym	Opportunities are there but they have to be worked for first.
Worm	sym	The earth's energy. Earth mysteries.

X

X-ray	sym	Unseen forces are at work. Changes are to be expected.
Xylophone	sym	Keep in tune with life and others.

Y

Yawn	sym	An outlet is needed from a boring situation.
Yeast	sym	Let nature and time take their course.
Yellow	sym	Sunshine and relief from burdens shortly.
Yew Tree	sym	There is nothing that can be done to alter facts.
Young	sym	Life and energy give hope for the future.

Z

Zebra	sym	There is a fifty-fifty chance of success.
Zodiac	sym	Fame and fortune are in the balance.
Zoo	sym	The world populated with all the different natures of the human family.

INDEX